WORLDS OF
ARTHUR
KING ARTHUR IN HISTORY, LEGEND
AND CULTURE

'How Morgan Le Fay gave a shield to Sir Tristram.' *Drawing by Aubrey Beardsley for Malory's* Le Morte D'Arthur, 1885

WORLDS OF
ARTHUR
KING ARTHUR IN HISTORY, LEGEND AND CULTURE

FRAN AND GEOFF DOEL, TERRY LLOYD

TEMPUS

First published 1998

Tempus Publishing Limited
The Mill, Brimscombe Port,
Stroud, Gloucestershire, GL5 2QG
www.tempus-publishing.com

British Library Cataloguing in Publication Data.
A catalogue record for this book is available from the British Library.

ISBN 0 7524 3393 8

Typesetting and origination by Tempus Publishing Limited
Printed and bound in Great Britain

Contents

List of Illustrations

Text Illustrations

PART I:

ARTHUR'S PLACE IN HISTORY
TERRY LLOYD

Introduction

Rather than ask whether there was an Arthur we should ask *why* there was an Arthur.

For many people he is a myth; a figure of folklore and fantasy to be regarded no more seriously than a character in a child's storybook. Yet there is probably more substance to the man of Arthurian legend than there exists behind other more powerfully pervasive mythologies.

History constantly creates its demands but only infrequently does society respond adequately, producing the likes of Luther, Napoleon, Bismarck and Gorbachev. The circumstances of a time define the man who is needed to meet its crisis and almost all the epochal figures of history have the contemporaneous record to draw them for posterity.

But what of the man who met the crisis of a society on the cusp between order and possible anarchy? Who records him for posterity? For him we must search – and yet this hunt for evidence of him makes him no less real than one who had his own biographer.

So where do we look for this man who is so shadowy and yet so potent that he straddles ages and cultures? We start a long way back, in a Britain before Rome. Because when we come to search for Arthur, we will have to look into a society facing life where the old certainty of Rome is gone but where the links to its pre-Roman past have been irretrievably broken, leaving it groping for a cohesion by which to survive.

Introduction

1 Britannia: The Roman Province of Britain

BEFORE THE ROMANS CAME ...

Society in Britain before the Romans came was based on tribal territories. Flocks and herds were the mainstay of life, supplemented by some arable farming where the grain crop was the most important. In the highland areas, transhumance was practised.

Whether the ruler of each territory called himself king or prince, his control depended upon his capacity to impose himself on a turbulent tribal aristocracy. A weak ruler was a recipe for civil war and the predatory instincts of neighbouring rulers.

It was a society without towns. The largest place in any tribal area was the stronghold from which the chieftain ruled and where he dwelled with kin, servants, slaves and the armed retinue on which he depended to enforce his rule. It was a society with virtually no roads. The time-old trackways were the principal lines of travel – lines such as the Ridgeway which linked the east coast with the south.

A society without towns and roads was one where trade was not well-developed. Localised bartering and folk-gatherings were the basis of exchange, apart from the movement of foreign merchants along the trackways. Their influence was greatest in the richer south-east, closest to the short sea crossing to the continent. But this was not a society on the verge of anarchy. It was a vigorous one which did not need a centralised bureaucracy to function. Its army was assembled of free warriors responding to the chieftain's summons. Its justice was the dispensation of the assembled menfolk. Lacking a written language, its laws, like its folk memories, were transmitted orally from generation to generation.

Rome's centralising power hit this delicate balance with the force of a battering ram.

PAX ROMANA

Though Julius Caesar made two incursions into southern Britain, the conquest had to await the reign of Claudius and came in AD 43. The original intention may have been to conquer only lowland Britain but the hostility of the tribes at its fringes sucked Rome ever westwards and northwards in search of a stable frontier. This meant the incorporation of Wales and, after the failure to incorporate Scotland, resting the northern frontier on the line of Tyne and Solway – Hadrian's Wall.

Within the shield of sea and Wall, the Roman peace was established in the classical way, and one which transformed the shape of the part of Britain which today is England. Where the legions went, there went the roads. Marvels of engineering, they sliced across the conquered territory to provide rapid access for soldiers, administrators, merchants and travellers.

Along those highways were the towns. Some were the capitals Rome provided for the old tribal territories; others grew up in or near the sites where the army paused before moving to the frontier areas. Roman engineers laid out the towns along the familiar grid pattern, laid in water supplies and drained out the waste. They built the splendid municipal buildings which marked the centre of every Roman town and the public baths which became its social focus.

In the tribal capitals the Roman administration was located, including the judiciary and the tax collectors. For now it was the law supervised by Rome which prevailed and with a standing army and a bureaucracy came the need for taxation revenues to maintain them. All those towns needed a food supply, most of it drawn from the surrounding area. And those who brought their produce to market could find there the consumer goods of a sophisticated society. Town and country became interdependent. For those who grew wealthy in this new society, there were its comforts to be enjoyed and its opportunities to be exploited. On their estates they built and furnished villas in the Roman style. They educated their sons in the Roman way, for they saw the way to advancement was through conformity.

Thus the men who were once the tribal aristocrats became Romans and their tribal past was diluted until it was lost beyond memory. Even for the great mass of the folk whose lives were less touched by Romanisation, there was no avoiding its percolating effects. Their sense of tribal identity was further eroded when those who might have been their leaders made their own cultural change. That process was completed when, for fiscal reasons, the once tightly-controlled grant of Roman citizenship was given to all free men within the Empire. This tightened the new common bonds and finally broke the old ones. Only in the remote corners of the Empire did the old tribal identities persist – in Britain that meant Wales and the north. But even there they could not escape that greatest of all Romanising factors – the army.

THE MILITARY ARRAY

The garrison of Britannia was of a strength out of all proportion to its size and its strategic and economic value. There were never less than three legions here – nominally, 15,000 men. In addition there were at times more than 20,000 auxiliaries, of whom 12,000 manned Hadrian's Wall and its outposts. At times, there is estimated to have been a total military strength of between 35,000 and 40,000 men and this may be a conservative figure.

A legionary was a Roman citizen. He might not have married until his service, usually fifteen years, was completed and then at his discharge he would be given a plot of land if he wished to remain in the province where he had been serving. One of the ways in which Rome rooted its influence in new provinces was to settle groups of these time-expired veterans in and around a town. They provided a wholly Roman cultural base which gradually spread outwards. The veterans also provided a nucleus of men to fill the municipal offices which also played their part in Romanisation.

An auxiliary was a Roman subject who would be given citizenship at the end of his service, usually twenty-five years. Auxiliaries were raised and served as territorial units but, for security reasons, in the early Empire they were never stationed in their native province. For example, a cohort (500 men) from Dacia (modern Romania) was stationed on Hadrian's Wall.

The auxiliaries were the men who did the dirty work. Almost invariably they were used to open a battle and might well carry it through to a conclusion in the right circumstances. Only if the going became rough or a tactical strike was required would the Roman commander launch his legions, for not only were they expensive to train and maintain, their numbers were also less than the hordes of expendable subject peoples.

The grant of citizenship to all free men in the Empire in the third century blurred the distinction between auxiliary and legionary. Thereafter, Rome recruited barbarian soldiers from the fringes of the Empire to fill the role formerly allotted to the auxiliaries.

The disposition of the garrison of Britannia was a guide to the nature of the threats it faced. The bulk of the forces was in the north. The auxiliary garrison of Hadrian's Wall was supported by outpost forces to the north and more auxiliaries in the Pennine forts; the whole network was anchored by the legion (VI) based at York. In an emergency, the legion based at Chester (XX) could move up in support. The threat was fourfold. Firstly, the minor element was the danger of an uprising by the mountain people of the Pennines who, though conquered and garrisoned, remained unruly. It is probable that the building of Hadrian's Wall bisected their territory, for it would be unreasonable to expect a tribal boundary to fit neatly with a strategic boundary.

Secondly, there were the major threats, these lying north of the Wall itself. In the far north, beyond the Forth–Clyde line, were a people whom historians for convenience call the Picts. Their relentless hostility to Rome was, combined with the manpower demands of other Imperial frontiers, enough to cause the failure of attempts to set the northern frontier between Forth and Clyde.

Between the Picts and the Wall lay peoples who were either three tribes or three groupings of tribes. When Rome tried to set the frontier on the Forth–Clyde line the intention was to absorb this huge reservoir of hostile warriors, together with the fertile lowlands. Even when the attempt failed and the Wall frontier was resumed, as much as possible was done to Romanise the peoples immediately to its north. Outpost forts were built to provide early warning of danger and to allow constant patrolling of the wild and dangerous territory. But there was no taming these people and the threat always remained. Though the lowland tribes in turn acted as a barrier to the Picts, the latter sometimes instead came raiding by sea. Thus, fortifications were built to stretch southwards from the western end of the Wall and signal stations were erected along the eastern coast below the Wall.

Thirdly, a lesser and more sporadic threat to the province came from Irish raiders. Auxiliary forts in Wales guarded against these and when the situation required they could be reinforced by men of the legion at Caerleon in south Wales (II) or the one at Chester. The latter also covered the threat posed by Irish raids across to what is now Lancashire and Cumbria, for the coastal defences were aimed at them as well as Picts striking south from Argyll.

Fourthly, and most ominous of all for Rome; a new threat began to emerge from the end of the second century and one which was symptomatic of the great danger which would eventually bring the Empire to its knees. Starting with small-scale raids, Germanic tribesmen from the North Sea coast began attacking Gaul and Britannia. History calls these raiders Saxons. It is doubtful that their maritime capabilities were such that they could regularly make direct strikes at Britannia from their homeland, though a few almost certainly did. Most of them probably hugged the coasts down to the narrows of the Channel and from there pressed on down into Gaul or cut across to Britannia.

Their usual method was to come in through a river mouth and get as far upstream as they could before carrying out their raid and darting back out to sea. The fleet based at Boulogne was not big enough to cover the amount of vulnerable coastline and so the governors of Britannia had to resort to static defence. The Roman fighting tradition believed the best form of defence was attack and so this new defensive system marked a significant stage in the Roman military decline.

Thus came into existence a series of coastal defences along what is known as the Saxon Shore, stretching from the Wash to Portsmouth. River mouths were guarded by new forts manned by auxiliaries which were intended to deny the raiders easy access but which could never completely block them. Eventually there came into existence another element of the Roman military response. A mobile force of cavalry and infantry was raised which would respond to an alarm and move to deal with intruders who evaded the defences of the Saxon Shore. It is a mark of the importance which Rome attached to this area, as well as an indication of the scale of the danger, that the commander of this force was the senior officer in the province.

Proving ever more critical for the governors of Britannia, was the fact that they had to meet the new threat of the Saxons without any additional resources and that could only compromise their other defence areas.

THE GATHERING STORM

Rome broke the tribalism of Celtic Britain with the iron claw of its uniformity. It protected its Romanised province with a massive military array which absorbed most, if not all, of Britannia's revenue. There was peace, and a prosperity which reached down through Romano-British society, though clearly – as with any societies – some benefited more than others. The latter were the ones with the greatest interest in ensuring life continued with minimal change.

And for Britannia, so for the entire Empire: from Hadrian's Wall to the Euphrates; from the Rhine-Danube frontier to the North-African deserts. But this seemingly secure world was under threat and the apparent invincibility of Rome was facing an ever-growing challenge.

From the second century AD the Germanic tribes of northern Europe began to migrate and in doing so they created ever-increasing pressure on the long Rhine-Danube frontier of the Empire. The reasons for the movements are not entirely clear but their impact is only too visible on the historical landscape. There was a domino effect – lesser tribes were pushed aside, knocking into others and thus in turn creating further dislocations. This enormous pressure upon the frontiers was not in itself catastrophic. Sometimes a section of the defences would crack, a savage incursion would follow and then with a great effort the legions would regain the frontier line and repair the damage. Sometimes intelligence reports would warn Rome of impending attack and a pre-emptive strike would be launched, a butchery and devastation aimed at crippling the capacity of the tribes to assault the frontier.

Even on Rome's north-west frontier there was a sinister development, for Britannia's sea frontiers could not shield her from the effect of the folk-wanderings. Along the North Sea coast of Germany the living conditions created a crisis. It may have been a simple growth in population or it may have been climatic changes resulting in a rise in the sea level. Either way it created a problem of insufficient land which in turn became critical because the tribes living there could not migrate south or east. The Rhine frontier of the Empire was holding back a great block of tribes who in turn barred the movement of the people along that coast. Other expanding tribal groupings barred their movement eastwards.

So they took to the sea and became known to the Romans of Gaul and Britannia as Saxons. Their raids were savage enough to lead to the erection of Britannia's coastal defences and the mobile response force already mentioned. But she, like the rest of the northern frontier, adjusted and seemed able to cope with the attacks. Then out of the east came the horsemen. The first wave, and perhaps the most terrible, was the Huns. Smashing into the German tribes, they knocked them westwards and in doing so cracked open the eastern end of the Danube frontier. Although the end would be long-delayed, this was the final crisis of the old Roman Empire. When it was over, the eastern half would begin a brilliant flowering as the Byzantine Empire but the bulk of the Empire of the Caesars would be gone.

The cracking of the eastern frontier only increased the pressure on the west, for the onslaught of the Huns sent shockwaves across Europe as tribes migrated away from them.

STRAWS IN THE WIND

Because the Roman Empire was a military dictatorship, it was susceptible to coups whenever external danger threatened and was not quickly and effectively met. Even in settled times an ambitious commander might suborn his legions and make his own bid for the purple. And sometimes the impetus even came from the legions themselves, demanding greater rewards for facing the ever-increasing dangers of frontier defence and mutinying if the demands were not met.

Britannia produced her share of pretenders, men who pared down the garrison beyond a reasonable safety threshold in order to take an army across to the continent to fight for the imperial throne. On each occasion the enemies of the province took full advantage. The western defences were always stripped first, for the Irish threat was perceived as the least dangerous and Wales was economically the least important part of the province. But, for reasons obscured from historians, the conditions in Ireland impelled some of the raiders to start settling in the western fringes of Wales where they would not face retaliation from the thinned-down garrison. In what is now Dyfed and Gwynedd, settlers put down roots and slowly their settlements began to expand. A similar process, on a smaller scale, was beginning in what is now north Devon and Cornwall. But stripping the western garrisons would not provide enough troops for a pretender and so the northern garrisons were also thinned. Given that a full complement could barely contain the northern peoples it is unsurprising that archaeology shows the Wall to have been breached on each occasion when a governor tried to become an emperor. The lowland tribes and the Picts came pouring through the gaps they made, sometimes just raiding in the north but on one occasion reaching almost to London.

Each time, it took a major effort to restore the frontier and subdue the tribes. Only the Saxon Shore was immune to the demands of the pretenders, for here was now the greatest danger and one which afflicted the wealthiest part of the province. The north and the west were, in the last resort, expendable but not only was the south the power base of any pretender, it was also home to the richest and most influential men of the province without whose support he dared not launch his bid. If, therefore, we look at Britannia's shield at the end of the third century AD and during the fourth, we see:

A northern frontier holding firm but still requiring a powerful garrison; A western frontier increasingly relegated in importance and nibbled at by Irish settlers whom the reduced garrison could not evict, and; A Saxon Shore defence taking greater priority as the sea raids grew in scale and intensity, with the mobile force using the road system to strike at those evading the security net.

What we also see – and it is of the utmost significance in the Arthurian quest – is that the fate of Britannia rested in the hands of its soldiers. The senior commander of the Roman forces in the province had absolute control and was no longer co-equal with other officials. The military solution was the one to which all else is bent. The commander at York and the commander of the Saxon Shore defences were high-ranking officers, but were out-ranked by the commander of the mobile strike force.

It was a defensive system barely equal to the triple pressures placed upon it and it took only the slightest diminution of the military array to create catastrophe. But even that tough shell protecting Britannia had flaws unnoticed by the imperial rulers. However, we have the wisdom of hindsight and it would be harsh of us to be too critical of the Roman authorities, right across the Empire, who were driven to adopting measures which contained the seeds of destruction.

A discourse on Rome's decline, especially the economic aspect, is a major work in its own right. For our purposes we must just work from the recognition that stagnation and inflation took an inevitable toll, even in a society as pragmatic and flexible as Rome's.

One result was diminished revenues which impaired the capacity to pay for the upkeep of the army. This coincided with an inexorable increase in the pressures generated by Rome's external foes. Unpaid soldiers meant mutiny, so the decision was taken to provide part of their pay by giving them plots of land near their station which would allow them, with their unofficial family (remember, they could not legally marry while serving), to grow food and sell the surplus.

One of the great strengths of the legionary system had been its flexibility. The men had no ties at their garrison post and could leave at very little notice for another part of the Empire. But men who hold land will not readily leave it and that attitude would have been reinforced now that the authorities, in giving them their plots, were in fact (though not in law) recognising the relationships contracted by the soldiers. Nothing was more likely to replace flexibility with immobility.

Another lapse in the military system had a similar effect. There had been a gradual shift away from the insistence that auxiliaries serve outside their own province and it accelerated when citizenship was freely granted. Now not only did the soldiers own land, but those soldiers were often native to the province where the land had been granted. What incentive would there have been for a group of such men to willingly leave the province for service elsewhere? However, this did ensure there would be a force of trained men on their native soil when the crisis came.

There was another strand to the defensive policy of the imperial rulers of the fourth century, and it was one which would have sinister consequences, both for Britannia and other provinces. The military manpower of the province was no longer adequate and so Germanic tribesmen, often prisoners of war, were settled in certain areas where they were given land to farm in return for military service. At the time when the policy was instituted, these pockets were no threat to the authorities because they were surrounded by much larger forces of imperial troops and could be suppressed easily if they mutinied. As the various threats to the Empire became greater in the late fourth and early fifth centuries, more and more troops were withdrawn from the remoter provinces, such as Britannia, to defend the heart of the Empire. More and more of these Germanic serf-soldiers were drafted in to fill the gaps.

CRISIS AND CATASTROPHE

The relentless pressure of the Germanic tribes on the Rhine-Danube frontier seemed containable but the situation was a delicately-balanced one, and it would take little to destabilise it completely. Unseen by any, that element was approaching from the steppes – the Huns, whose shattering impact has already been mentioned and whose arrival heralded the break-up of the Roman Empire.

There was an irony for Britannia in all this. She was enjoying a last period of prosperity after enduring one awful agony in the middle of the fourth century when it seemed she would be smothered by the weight of her enemies. Contemporary historians called it 'the barbarian conspiracy' and there did seem to be a scent of co-ordination about the combined assault by the Irish, Picts, lowland tribes and Saxons. Assailed from three sides at once, the Roman army was engulfed, its senior commanders killed and only the strength of its fortifications saved it from utter disaster. But the tide ebbed and a renewed effort restored the frontiers and breathed new life into the province. While the rest of the Empire was battered and its eastern part was torn, this north-western frontier enjoyed a last flowering, though the enemies still prowled.

During this period there was one incident which should be recorded here because of its future significance. Towards the end of the century the senior Roman commander in Britannia made a bid to be emperor and, though he came surprisingly close to success, failed at a battle in the Balkans. Part of his army set off for home, but in Gaul was offered extensive coastal lands to settle if it could root out the nests of pirates. The incessant attentions of the Saxons had turned parts of the northern coasts of Gaul – like parts of the eastern coast of Britannia – into debatable land where few would risk living. The home-bound men of Britannia were willing to use their fighting skills to take on the risks in return for land and they settled along the rocky fringes of the Armorican coast. When Gaul eventually fell into Germanic hands, this isolated Celtic territory would become known as *Bretannia*: Brittany.

The province which they had left as part of a usurper's army was about to spawn another emperor, though for entirely different reasons. The paring away of Britannia's garrison could only encourage the predators who ringed the province, but there was more at work here than just a thinned-down defensive system failing to meet its purpose. Many of the men being marched off to defend the Rhine or Danube frontier, or fight in Italy itself, were not the legionaries of old whose sole obedience was to their eagles. These were men born in Britannia, with land to farm and families to defend against the renewed attacks of raiders encouraged by reduced defences. Why should they march off to fight for the survival of others in a remote place which meant nothing to them while their own land was ravaged?

With the encouragement of Britannia's leading men, the army defied orders and made its commander, Constantine, an emperor. But he was given the purple not that he might rule an empire but so that he might rule in the province. His Empire was to be Britannia and they would follow him in defending it, their homeland. Within the fortifications of the north and the Saxon Shore, the mobile force of cavalry and infantry which he commanded would deal with the centuries-old threats whenever they evaded the defensive network. And the usual resources of the provinces would be available to maintain this army. Roman life would continue without Rome.

The year was 406.

IMPERIAL TWILIGHT

The written evidence about the fate of Britain now begins to dwindle towards the blank page. We do know something of events between AD 406 and 410 but thereafter we have to fall back on inferences drawn from what are asides in contemporary chronicles from other places, on archaeology, and on oral traditions which were committed to writing much later.

In AD 407 the ultimate catastrophe befell the western Roman Empire which had relied for so long on the river barrier of the Rhine supplemented by garrisons on the left bank. On the last night of AD 406, the Rhine froze and across the ice came the Germanic tribesmen to engulf the meagre forces left to hold the river defences. The Gallic provinces were wasted as they had never been wasted before by rampaging tribesmen who reached the Channel coast before turning away southwards. This disaster not only severed the most northerly of Rome's provinces from the Imperial administration, it also provoked in Constantine the ambition of a wider domain. Looking at the ruin of Roman Gaul, he decided to use his troops to take advantage of the chaos across the water. He crossed with all the forces he could raise in the hope of taking control as the tribesmen moved away southwards.

Just what forces he took is unclear. The mobile force directly under his command would undoubtedly have gone and if any forces remained in Wales he probably stripped them out. We can make no safe assumptions about what he did with the garrisons of the Saxon Shore. However, it can reasonably be inferred that he took little of the northern garrison. The north was controlled by the commander at York whose men were probably almost all natives of the province, farming land near their station. They would have a natural aversion to adventures which left their homes defenceless in the face of the ancient enemies. Besides, the commander at York had no reason to weaken his garrisons to help a colleague, even one nominally his superior, in a hazardous act of self-aggrandisement.

We know that Constantine was initially successful but then overreached himself and was betrayed to his death. But even before that, disaster had struck Britannia. The nature of it is unknown but the history of the province suggests an increase in raids by the Irish and the Saxons (the northern threat being contained by the commander at York). But whatever its shape, we know it was of such a magnitude that the leading men of the province abandoned Constantine just as they felt he had abandoned them. After AD 407 their situation became so dire that, in 410, they appealed directly to the legitimate Emperor, Honorius, for help.

Clearly, Constantine had so stripped down the southern forces in the province that the remaining troops could no longer deal with the onslaught. His ambition had imperilled the province which only created him emperor in a desperate search for security. He was now rejected for his failure and the province sought to return to its loyalty. But Honorius had acute problems of his own. From the safety of Ravenna in northern Italy he was watching the Gothic army of Alaric moving on Rome and there was nothing his commanders could do about it. If he could not defend the old Imperial capital, much less could he spare men for the furthest province. Instead he bade the citizens of Britannia look to their own resources 'until the Imperial authorities were in a position to restore the links and provide succour'. It is at this point we lose full sight of Romano-British history. Somewhere in the darkness beyond is Arthur and to find him we have to draw on evidence which is circumstantial and from which we are forced to draw inferences, as well as construct theories.

THE ROMAN BEQUEST

Before wandering off into this murk, let us first look at where we are starting. Rome had ruled Britannia for a little over 350 years. One of her great strengths was her eclecticism, the willingness to adopt and to absorb elements of another people's culture if it proved expedient or advantageous to do so. But even when she did that, it was in an inimitably Roman way which transmuted what was absorbed to render it acceptable within the Roman ethos. The product was an indelible footprint.

Only in the remotest areas did a man now say he belonged to this tribe or that. He was a citizen of the Roman province and his place of origin was the capital of the territory in which he lived. That territory probably coincided with the tribal area of the conquest but there is no indication that it survived as such in folk memory. From that town the citizen was governed. If he had a law suit, he took it there; if he committed a crime, he would be judged there. He paid his taxes there. If he was entitled to a voice in the elections of those who carried out the administration, it was cast there.

As imperial government began to decay, the system of patronage received a sharp stimulus. It profited lesser men to throw in their lot with those who were wealthier and more powerful. This client relationship afforded protection to the lesser man and gave him extra weight in court; in return, his sword and voice were at the disposal of his patron. Since the town was the focus of government, the wealthiest would maintain a presence there, even if their principle residence was the country estate from which their wealth was derived. We could even say the old tribal chieftainates were being recreated but those who wielded the power saw themselves not as tribal lords but as magistrates of Rome. They operated an administrative system which, despite all the pressures placed on it, still functioned. But even if it failed, what were they going to put in its place? They knew only what they and ten generations before them knew: the Roman way. And it worked.

Protecting them was a Roman army. It might lack the menacing might of the legions at their peak but it was still formidable: well-armed, highly-disciplined and with centuries of tradition binding it. Even in the death-throes of an empire, in battle after battle from Rhine-mouth to the Black Sea, the Roman army remained formidable and when it died, it died hard.

The military and administrative machines were paid for by taxation and even when stagnation and decline reduced the tax yield, Roman ingenuity and pragmatism found ways of covering the gap. By allotments of land and payment in kind, combined with some hard cash, they kept the machinery working and, as the Empire collapsed, those expedients were remembered.

BRITANNIA WITHOUT ROME

Britannia at the end of imperial rule could be divided into three areas:

1   The north: from the Wall down to perhaps the Humber in the east and Chester in the west, a substantial military force protected the small farms which, with some large estates, were the backbone of economic life. This area was controlled by the commander at York.

2   The west: the interior of Wales was probably reverting to some kind of tribalism, with Irish colonists taking a grip along the western coast. Life here lacked any central control, apart from the areas around Chester, Wroxeter (near modern Shrewsbury), Gloucester and Caerleon.

3   Elsewhere, in what was the wealthiest part of the province, small farms mingled with large estates focused on villas. The greatest concentration of towns was here and most of the industry.

The south was protected from the oldest enemies by the bulwark of the northern command. It had the Saxon Shore defences to cope with the newest enemies. It was content for the Irish to settle at the extremes of Wales and to nibble away at the remoter parts of Devon and Cornwall.

There was no central control down here but the most powerful men probably came together in a council intended originally for religious purposes associated with the worship of the Imperial divinity. It may have been this assembly which made the appeal to Honorius in AD 410 and it was the same men who took him at his word by finding the means to defend themselves. We have no clues as to how they achieved their breathing space but contemporaries on the continent alluded to their success. There is no reason to think they regarded their actions as anything other than an *interregnum* until Rome resumed control. We have history to tell us that Rome was never coming back but all their traditions led them to expect it. Each time a usurper had launched his bid from Britannia there had been dislocation of links with Rome, sometimes for years, but always they were restored. So now the men who controlled southern Britain did as their emperor commanded and awaited the return to normality.

It never came. Our hunt for Arthur is their search for another normality.

2 Into the Darkness

When next we clearly see Britannia it is after 150 years have passed. Its eastern part had started to become England. Germanic kingdoms had emerged. Their social, economic and political structure was completely different from that left behind by Rome. During that obscured century and a half, the Britannia created and bequeathed by Rome has clearly failed and that failure contains the matter of Arthur.

To search for him we must rely on archaeology and on inferences from written sources. Few of the latter are contemporary and those which are do not deal directly with Britain. But there is a trail to be followed. It is that left by the men we might call the Warlords of Britain.

The First of the Warlords

Within a decade of the vain appeal by the southern leaders to Honorius, the success achieved by their own efforts was in jeopardy.

FAMILIAR FOES

The withdrawal of all garrisons in Wales had seen an expansion of the Irish settlements. The Irish colonies in north Devon and Cornwall also spread. This activity coincided with a further upsurge in raiding from Ireland itself, much of it directed up through the Bristol Channel to strike into the Cotswolds and Wiltshire which was the wealthiest part of Britain.

The Pictish activity was probably stimulated by the various kingdoms north of the Forth–Clyde line being united under a single strong ruler who then directed the restlessness of his warriors beyond his frontiers. The northern frontier of the province was still holding at the Wall which meant that the lowland tribesmen were being contained, though it is clear they were exerting extreme pressure on the post-Roman forces. So the Picts resumed their habit of bypassing both the tribesmen and the Wall defences by taking to the sea.

The signal stations running south from the Wall along the east coast

ensured warning of the raiders who then pressed on further south towards the richer areas which they could get into along the road network.
The commander at York was unlikely to use his forces to chase after them
provided they did not land in his area. He would leave the southerners to
look after themselves. He would owe them nothing because it is unlikely
he was still getting material support from the south. The administrative
divisions of the late Roman province were hardening into separate territories and York was taking on the mantle of a territorial ruler.

If the Saxon threat was, as it seems, either absent or diminished during this particular crisis it was probably the result of the chaos in Gaul
which meant easier and richer pickings there. The renewal of the Irish
and Pictish activity suggests the raiders knew that inroads were possible
which in turn implies the defences were weaker. We can safely assume
that, whatever the nature of the measures taken to deal with the threat
a decade before, they incurred unacceptable costs and it is there that we
ought to look for the problem.

THE BURDEN OF DEFENCE

The burden of paying for security fell on the wealthiest men of the south
and when the threat receded there would have come a point where the
cost would no longer seem justified. The very absence of danger would
create the illusion of safety, as it does throughout history.

There is a further point in this. The parts of southern Britannia most
exposed to raiders were the east coast and the West Country's northern
shores. The wealthiest parts of the south were the Cotswolds and the
Wiltshire-Hampshire-Dorset area which lay at the extreme range of the
raiders' reach. So those of the British with the most capacity to pay were
the ones least threatened and so, with the passage of time, they would become less and less inclined to fund the defences which mainly benefited
others. This period of history is by no means alone in demonstrating such
myopia. The suggestion that it was a cost-based problem is given strength
by what happened next.

MILITARY MIGHT

In the early 420s it seems a power struggle took place within the ruling
elite and when the dust settled a single individual had emerged to take
control of the military situation. He is of the utmost significance to us
because the path he marks will lead to Arthur. History and myth call this

man Vortigern. That was not his name but his title. The Romano-Celtic language (the pre-Roman tongue heavily influenced by Latin) was now shaping into proto-Welsh and 'Vortigern' is a corruption of an Early Welsh term for a warlord with wide powers. His origins and his road to power are unknown. He was probably not one of the ruling elite but a warrior used by them to deal with a military problem. Somewhere along the way the servant became virtual master.

He first addressed the Irish problem. Clearly a capable and long-sighted man, he recognised that abandoning the furthest reaches of the west to Irish settlers was not an option. Those areas might not matter to the men who held the purse strings but Vortigern knew that eventually they would become the source of great difficulties. Indeed, the Irish settlements in Wales were already expanding rapidly eastwards.

One area of particular pressure was in north-east Wales and Vortigern adopted a twin-track approach here which in turn affected his solution to the Irish problem in north Devon and Cornwall. He encouraged the migration of a people from where the Welsh hill country met the lowlands of Shropshire. These were the Cornovii who moved to attack the Irish settlements in the West Country and would eventually give their name to Cornwall. Too few in numbers to deal with the Irish in Wales, they were enough to uproot those in north Devon. Into their place he brought some of the tribesmen from the lowlands to the north of Hadrian's Wall. The easternmost group of these tribes, the Votadini, were caught as they had been for centuries between the restlessly aggressive Picts and the unyielding frontier of Rome. Population growth was creating its own additional pressures and it was either this, or some civil strife within the Votadini, which led to a large number of the warriors and their families migrating to north Wales.

We are looking here at a massive undertaking. It would have required the co-operation of the ruler at York who clearly had a vested interest in easing the pressures on one corner of his frontier but who must have swallowed hard before allowing such an influx to be shepherded diagonally along the length of his territory. To Cunedda, the leader of these people, Vortigern made a simple offer: 'the land you need is there to be taken from the Irish'. From the eastern parts of north Wales, right across to the Lleyn peninsula there was fighting to be done and he reckoned he was diverting a dangerous northern foe into a long war to deal with an even more dangerous enemy.

He was right. Cunedda and his descendants were the founders of the dynasties which ruled north and west Wales for centuries after they had subdued the Irish. Vortigern drew on Roman practice when he devised these moves. He was aware such strategies had been used by the Imperial authorities for centuries. Just a piece more of Britain's Roman heritage was being deployed.

His other move also drew on Roman practice. Ever since the Germanic tribes had been rampaging across the ruins of the Empire, different rulers had resorted to using one tribe or another as what were called *federati*. In return for attacking a ruler's enemy (sometimes other Germanic tribes), the *federati* were given land to settle as subjects and were also given provisions, usually in the form of grain, until they were established. Although much of the Saxon activity had been diverted away from Britain towards richer pickings, some of it continued and it looks as though a small contingent may have been using an isolated corner as a base. This group, probably of mixed origins rather than from the same tribe, was led by an adventurer called Hengest who seems to have made himself unwelcome in the area of modern Netherlands/Belgium. He had been dabbling there in the strife of the post-Roman rulers and made himself so unwelcome that he and his warband found it safer to find other work.

The Isle of Thanet in modern Kent offered them a piece of coastline from which to sail on their raids, while at the same time giving them a measure of protection to the landward. Vortigern saw a chance to deploy them as *federati* for dealing with the Pictish threat and made them an offer – Thanet and grain supplies in return for their swords and their ships. He intended to control them and use them, regarding their numbers as too small to pose threat but enough to do the necessary fighting. It worked. The Pictish threat ended, though whether by fighting or simply because of the appearance of a strong defence, we do not know.

By the middle of the 420s, Vortigern's strategy had achieved his objectives. Irish and Pictish threats were nullified, the northern commander somewhat indebted because the pressure on him was eased, and Vortigern's own power had been enormously enhanced. Not only did he have a group of *federati* at his command but he had also given the rulers of the south security without incurring vast expense. There would be the upkeep of some soldiers – that was unavoidable – and the cost of provisioning the *federati*, but all in all the price of security was not great. He also had some native soldiers, probably through a quota system from each of the little territories into which the south was dividing and it is reasonable to assume they were used in much the same way that the mobile force of the late Empire was deployed: moving at speed to meet any threat which penetrated the outer screen. Yet it seems even this comparatively small cost was too great.

CIVIL WAR

While the rest of post-Roman Europe was convulsed and ravaged, Britannia experienced a decade of calm but this ended suddenly when internecine warfare erupted in the south. Vortigern fought with an opponent called Ambrosius but we are left in the dark as to whether the latter was a new rival or an old one making a return. Certainly, he might have returned from exile in Brittany where many of the British had links with those early settlers (see above).

The battle was inconclusive, leaving each man to fall back among his supporters. Vortigern's were in the east where he also had his *federati* under Hengest. Ambrosius's were in the west which raises the prospect that the cause of this war might again have been the cost of security measures. The principal beneficiaries of the peace were those dwelling in the eastern part of the country while the main wealth was to be found in the west. Ambrosius would have found willing supporters for a proposal to let those who needed protection pay for it.

There now came an event which caused those generations immediately after Vortigern to vilify him and cast him into the demonology of legend for having invited in Hengest and his warband.

THE SEEDS OF ENGLAND

In recruiting those *federati*, Vortigern followed best practice of the late- and post-Empire but hindsight shows what he did was loose the wolf within the sheepfold. His great misfortune was to lack hindsight.

For Hengest now attacked him. While Vortigern was preoccupied with Ambrosius his rear was assailed by the men he assumed to be his subject-allies. Hengest could not but have been aware of instances where Germanic warrior chieftains had seized power from the feeble hands of Rome's successors. Some even went on to control the later shadowy Emperors. Now he saw his chance to emulate them. Not only had Vortigern's power been slashed with the loss of the west, but now he had to use his remaining strength to fend off his rival, Ambrosius. That loss of the west also deprived Vortigern of part of the means to fulfil the bargain with the *federati*: the grain supply. That in itself would have offered Hengest a quasi-legitimate excuse for hostilities on the grounds that the contract was broken.

Who knows whether such a nicety was deployed. What we do know is that a ferocious attack out of Kent took Vortigern by surprise, scattering his forces and continuing on westwards as a massive raid. The raiders were too few in numbers to effect a conquest, even if they were considering it, and eventually they ebbed back into the settlement areas with their loot. In the process they caused enough dislocation to hope they would be left undisturbed in possession of their land, answerable now to none and in a position in good time to think about expansion.

We need to consider at this point the possibility that Hengest's warriors might have been joined by others from further north in what is now East Anglia. Mention has already been made of the Germanic serf-soldiers and we have to consider the possibility that their descendants heeded an appeal by the wily Hengest. With Rome's power withered and no control on them, the settlers would see the chance to do more than protect the area – they could take control of it. They would have been assisted in this by the decay of the elaborate drainage system by which the Romans had reclaimed part of the Fens. Once the water started to regain control it would have created a natural barrier from behind which they could operate with virtual impunity.

Whether it was a single assault out of Kent, or a two-pronged offensive including the East Anglians, it attracted retribution. Once Vortigern recovered from the shock and damage of the attack, he turned on his erstwhile allies, for he could not countenance such a dangerous precedent. Hengest would not have expected to be left in peace after he made his strike but he must have looked at the odds and decide he could beat off the retaliation. Perhaps he calculated that Ambrosius would also turn on Vortigern and thus fatally handicap him.

In fact, Hengest miscalculated on two counts. Firstly, Ambrosius did not make any further attack on Vortigern. He was probably content with removing the west of the province from the effects of the turmoils of the east. Secondly, the retaliation was more powerful than Hengest expected. Led by Vortigern's sons or protégés, the British forces fought a prolonged war which may have lasted as long as a decade and that was as much to do with the reduced forces available to Vortigern's men as the level of resistance from the settlers. But the upshot was that Hengest was driven from Kent. Either his warriors left with him or some or all came to heel.

Hengest seems to have slipped away to East Anglia where he could find refuge among the settlers there. Vortigern had focused his limited resources on the obvious danger in Kent, leaving the settlers in East Anglia unmolested in their fastness. It is likely that new migrants from Germany were already filtering into this area, swelling the numbers of the original settlement families. A formidable warrior force was growing here.

Now Vortigern received overtures from Hengest. Probably assuming the ingrate had learned his lesson and was suitably contrite, Vortigern agreed to a meeting where he would expect Hengest to resume his federate role. No doubt Vortigern intended to use his federates on Ambrosius – he was after all successor to the Roman commander and so responsible for all the south of Britannia. No arms were to be carried at the meeting but Hengest and his men came with concealed weapons which they used to surprise and butcher Vortigern's supporters. Vortigern himself was not killed but was kept alive to cloak Hengest's actions with some kind of legality. Again, the intruder was following in the footsteps of other Germanic leaders who had taken control in parts of the post-Roman world without taking a throne or a title. Vortigern now passes from the scene – the first of the warlords has gone.

The slaughter of their leaders left the British exposed to yet another onslaught. If some of the Kent men had indeed submitted, they doubtless took the opportunity to throw off the yoke. The East Anglians took the chance to widen their grip and ease the pressure of a growing population. The British living in the eastern part of the province had suffered centuries of raiding and had learned to cope with it but those batterings left the economy fragile, a situation worsened by the renewal of the Fens. Now the proximity of a barbarian settlement area, coupled with this outbreak of savagery, proved too much for those closest to the seat of the danger. Many migrated, some towards the sanctuary of the West but others went right away from the danger. They crossed the sea to Lesser Britain – Brittany – where others of their people had found safety.

But many of the British remained in eastern Britain. Those with the most to lose took their wealth and sought a fresh start. Those with less to lose, and perhaps even something to gain, clung to their land and fought for a living in this precarious frontier district. The towns gave them refuge in times of crisis because the raiders were unskilled in siege warfare. And into this war zone came Ambrosius.

The Second of the Warlords

A ROMAN ARMY?

Ambrosius now saw the futility and the danger of the policy of either leaving Vortigern to deal with the settlers or of abandoning the eastern area to them. His sudden awareness might have been born of an awakening to just what was loose within the province, or his links with the continent might have alerted him to what was happening in the areas where the Germanic peoples had settled: they were taking over. With forces from the west and centre of southern Britain, he came against the settlers. It is reasonable to assume he had a mixture of volunteers and men levied from the areas into which the province was splintering. From each of the larger towns the surrounding territory was ruled by a single powerful individual or a small group. Because it was in their interests to root out the settlers, they would have been willing – albeit reluctantly – to provide men and resources for Ambrosius.

Post-Roman Britain had reached once more for her Roman heritage. In an economy no longer cash-based, its political élite found men, mounts, equipment and provisions to enable a chosen commander to wage war. And no doubt a small amount of coin would be found for the soldiers who would follow the man chosen to command this Roman army. And in the tradition of the mobile force which was the backbone of the final Imperial garrison, it was cavalry backed up by infantry which now bore down on the settlers. The Romano-British intended to uproot these Germanic barbarians and drive them back into the sea from which they came. They penned them into the settlement areas from which they had broken free but were then confronted with the bitter fact that ultimate success was out of reach.

THE BITTER REALITY

The settler numbers had grown considerably. Some of the warriors of the 450s/early 460s facing Ambrosius's men would have been born in the settlements in Kent or East Anglia. They too had families and in a society where a male came of fighting age at fourteen there was an ever-increasing pool of warriors. In addition to this natural increase, a constant trickle of immigration swelled their numbers.

Sooner or later, the course of the fighting must have shown the British that it was virtually impossible to drive out the settlers and so a policy was adopted of making the greatest possible inroads into their territory and then planting strongholds at strategic places. This provided a constant watch on the settlers to allow warning of any attempt to break new ground or to launch an attack. With a strong population growth, this policy must ultimately result in starvation or migration.

It is perhaps appropriate now to start referring to the settlers as the English – not because they would have recognised the term but because it is a convenient shorthand for us which also recognises that the birth of successive generations renders the term 'settlers' obsolete.

AMBROSIAN WARFARE

The Ambrosian war was waged intermittently over perhaps twenty years. What little we know of Ambrosius suggests he had been born into the provincial aristocracy, perhaps related to one of the men who had made a bid for the imperial throne during Britannia's lifetime. No doubt it was this background which allowed him to assume the mantle of warlord, perhaps using some of his own wealth as well as his status to place himself to the fore. But the fact of his success indicates ability as well as rank.

The kind of war he waged would not have been the perpetual campaigning we know from twentieth-century wars, but one fought on a seasonal basis and not necessarily annually. He would not take the field until long enough after winter for his men and mounts to regain their strength and the spring grass be thick enough to graze his horses. At least some of his men would have farms of their own and so the spring ploughing would need to be over before they would muster. And they would want to be home by harvest-time. There would be some years when the English would show no aggression – perhaps after a bad harvest or when disease thinned their numbers – and so no campaign was required.

One has to wonder how many times during a quiet season the men whose purses bore the strain of the war thought once more of standing down at least part of the army. Did they perhaps forget the lessons learned so harshly earlier in the century? But if they did, then Ambrosius must have sharply reminded them, for it is clear the pressure remained on the English and he could not have done that without the support of the men whose army he led. Then sometime around the period AD 470-480, Ambrosius died – the second of the warlords had gone and we reach the critical point in a search for Arthur.

The Third of the Warlords

THE LEGACY

Vortigern's supremacy was the result of late-Roman Britain turning back to what it knew, having lately rejected it: a sole military commander to deal with a familiar menace. The first of the warlords addressed his problems with familiar Roman expedients, one of which backfired disastrously, though through no obvious error on his part.

The disaster leading to his downfall created a threatening situation which, in its similarity to remembered dangers, called for recourse yet again to the single military commander. So the second of the warlords again exercised sole command and was able to call on common resources to fight a common foe in order to preserve the only way of life the British knew or understood. It was the survival of the Roman way of life against the onset of barbarism in the shape of the Germanic tribesmen.

When Ambrosius's time was done the danger was still there. The settlers were contained and hemmed in but within those over-populated settlement areas there seethed the menace of a warrior people who were desperate for more land and had the strength to take it if the opportunity offered itself.

For the rulers of Britain the temptation to dispense with their expensive army must have been strong as Ambrosius's hand fell away. And their history suggests they would probably have grasped at the chance, willing to persuade themselves that the penned-in English were no longer a real danger. But the world was changing more rapidly than they could ever have expected.

THE GROWING PERIL

Three important developments occurred towards the end of the century.

Firstly, Clovis, the creator of the Frankish kingdom in Gaul, was smashing down all resistance, be it among his own people or by those who did not wish to become his subjects. Among his victims were the small groups of sea-borne raiders whose bases were along the coastline that Clovis was dragging into his kingdom. They were no longer welcome and their choice was submission or resettlement. At least one large group chose the latter and fastened its grip on a portion of southern England. Its leader is known to history as Aelle and the kingdom which would grow from his settlement would be known as that of South Saxons: Sussex.

Secondly, for reasons still obscure, there was now a last spasm of migration from the old homelands of the Germanic raiders. Out of what is now southern Denmark and northern Germany came the kings whose surplus populations had earlier been the source of so much grief and pain for late- and post-Roman Europe. Where their warriors had gone, now came the kings with the much of the remaining folk. Some – perhaps most – struck out for eastern Britain. But although some might have found a welcome in East Anglia, there was little if any surplus land in the old settlement areas. So the arrivals began seeking a foothold north of the Wash in Lincolnshire and in the marshy lands where the Trent entered the Humber. This created a whole new danger for the forces of the British. Clearly, the southern rulers now needed an accommodation with the ruler at York, for this abutted his own southern flank. But here lay the third development. The unified rule of the north was breaking up. At least two and probably three generations ruled from York after Rome left, either the same family or a succession of military commanders. But now York's grip was loosening, either because of an inadequate succession or simply because of the vigour of the men seeking to break free as rulers in their own right. The north was splintering into little princedoms.

For the men of the south this posed a pair of problems. A splintering north would provide little or no co-operation against the new waves of settlers. And, just as grave, the weight of those tribes north of Hadrian's Wall might now be able to break through. It might have been a long time since these had been able to launch a major invasion but Rome's successors knew their own history.

So Ambrosius died at a time when not only were the English still a considerable menace, but the whole political situation in the south and north and east became clouded and potentially dangerous. Even the doubters could see this was no time to be reducing their vigilance.

This was the greatest crisis to face Roman Britain that century and the moment produced a man who not only met it but overcame it and gave Britain a last flowering of calm and prosperity before disaster turned much of it into England.

IN DEFENCE OF AN INHERITANCE

The term 'Roman Britain' is used with calculation. For it was neither 'England' nor was it 'Britain': a Celtic tribal society. It was what historians call a Romano-British society which was no longer Roman but which used all that Rome bequeathed because it knew no other way to go.

The descendants of men who had been proud to call them magistrates of Rome were now calling themselves kings and princes, rulers over portions of what had been the Roman province. To the extent that they still had the resources, they lived in the style of their Romanised ancestors. They governed from within the towns Rome built and walled and they ruled by the institutions Rome left. They were protected by a force modelled on the army which had defended the province as the Empire crumbled, an army which still had that road network along which to operate. No longer maintained to the high standards of Roman engineers but built so well as still to be defying time and poor upkeep.

We are fairly sure that it was not one of these kinglets and princelings who now assumed Ambrosius's mantle, though he may have been drawn from the ranks of the island's aristocracy. It is the only thing we are sure about when we look for Arthur.

Of him we know absolutely nothing beyond the fact that he commanded the armed forces of the rulers of Britain but was not a king or prince himself. Even his name is a source of fertile debate – was it his given name or was it, like Vortigern, a title? The really concrete thing about Arthur is his achievement, which has survived through the folklore of the society from which he sprang. We know what preceded him and we know what followed him. But of a lifetime which created arguably the most potent figure of British history we know virtually nothing except what we can infer. Yet that lifetime created a legend among the British and excited medieval romancers from beyond the Celtic world into creating a myth which almost every generation since has used in its literature.

THE RULER OF BATTLES

It is a lifetime marked by battle. Arthur was no anointed monarch with the judicial, administrative and religious responsibilities and rights of a king. He was a warlord who commanded the forces of the British rulers as they fought off what to them were the forces of darkness, an enemy whose primitive way of life was inimical to all their traditions.

All we have of Arthur are those battles. And our only source for those battles is a document which itself has been the subject of intense debate as to its meaning and its accuracy. Beyond that debate is another – where are the places named in it? Not one of them is clear beyond doubt to the modern eye but a great deal of scholastic energy and ingenuity has been expended in identifying the battle sites. There is a degree of consensus among the scholars which enables us to say with some confidence that Arthur's campaigning ranged between modern Scotland and the west of England.

And that perhaps is why history and legend remember Arthur and not Ambrosius as the pivotal figure in the annals of Romano-Britain. Where Ambrosius fought against the early settlers in a limited part of southern Britain, Arthur faced a greater number of dangers over a greater range of the country.

The battle list shows much of his fighting to have been in the river valleys of eastern Britain. This is not surprising. The settlers coming from northern Europe would bring their ships into estuaries and then get as far upstream as they could, to where marsh or bog would afford them some protection from Arthur's horsemen. It is likely that some of the families from the old settled areas in East Anglia and Kent may have used the sea to break out in search of new homes because the horsemen and garrisons prevented them breaking out by land.

For it is certain they could not break the stranglehold imposed in Ambrosius's time. There is no indication of Arthurian battles being fought around Kent or East Anglia, though the northern fringes of the latter may have been caught up in his campaigns. Of the English, it was the new settlers who drew his attention.

But it was not just the English who confronted the warlord of the British. It is clear that some of his battles were fought in the far north and in the west – here we are looking at an old enemy or perhaps a sinister new development. In the north it would have been either the Picts or some combination involving the lowland tribes so hostile to Rome for so long. Tradition points to the Picts from north of the Forth–Clyde line and if that was the case then Arthur was clearly acting on behalf of the north British rulers. In order simply to survive they were giving up the independence cherished since the end of imperial rule. In the west the enemy might have been Irish raiders, renewing their depredations. Or it might have been some muscle-flexing by Cunedda's descendants who, protected by their mountains, were rejecting the terms on which they had been allowed to migrate.

MEN ON HORSEBACK

Although the Arthurian world of the medieval romances is a knightly one, we should not be misled into thinking this was just contemporary writers imposing their notion of warfare on to the past. Rather we should think of the accuracy of the Arthurian story making it easier for the medieval balladeers to fit him into their world of chivalry and courtly love. For Arthurian warfare was based on the horseman.

That fast-moving cavalry and infantry force of the late Empire was probably used by Vortigern and was almost certainly used by Ambrosius. Arthur could not have covered the ground that he did, campaigning from north to south, unless he too had a fast-moving force at his disposal. He had the decaying Roman road network to give him fast access into the threatened areas.

Britain was now ruled by princelings and kinglets, jealous of their autonomy but aware that alone they were nothing in the face of desperate settlers in search of land, or hostile northerners and wild Irish keen to loot their fertile lands. The rulers of Britain contributed men and mounts, weapons and provisions to keep their warlord in the field. When threatened by greater forces than their own levies could cope with, then they summoned the army of Arthur. They would not lightly call on him, for when he entered their territory with his forces they had to maintain them until the danger was past. He would come with his horsemen, moving quickly to the seat of the danger and if that proved to be too great for a small force, he would have to await the footmen hurrying up behind him. His forces would be supplemented for battle by the local levies but the weight of the fighting would fall on the professionals.

This was unlikely to be a war of cavalry charges. Arthur's horsemen might have ridden to battle and then either fought on foot or skirmished the enemy battle line. The stirrup had not yet revolutionised warfare and without its firmness there could be no charge at a solid shield-wall – even had it been possible to persuade horses to confront such a menacing formation. But even so the presence of the horsemen should not be under-estimated. There is well documented evidence of the fear and loathing inspired in the Germanic tribesmen by the presence of cavalry. The horsemen might not be able to thunder against the shield-wall of the settlers but they could prevent it opening out to become mobile. They could pin down a landing force, harass it and pick off any part of it which left the shelter of the mass. Then the full weight of the British force could give battle on foot and once the shield-wall was broken the horsemen could get in among the fleeing enemy.

Of course, horsemen are vulnerable when dismounted and so Arthur used the sheltering walls of those Roman towns as a base when he entered an area to campaign. The settlers had no siege equipment with which to storm any of the towns and so deny this relentless enemy a base from which to attack them.

And because horsemen are vulnerable when not on the move Arthur would have needed a base for his headquarters and winter quarters. Military practice suggests that at least part of his force would stand down each winter, returning to their homes and rejoining the colours with the approach of spring. But tactics and strategy (and even politics) would keep a substantial part of the force under arms throughout the year. Some of these men would have families who must be kept safe while they were in the field, families which would need to farm for subsistence.

All this points to a stronghold at a point remote from the danger of English attack, yet close enough to the hubs of the road network to get the army quickly into the field and moving on the latest threat. The towns would not be suitable: their walls would not be adequate for sustained military use; they would lack the interior space for a big force with horses and, more to the point, civilians are never comfortable with large numbers of soldiers in close proximity.

The Romans left only three legionary fortresses: York, Chester and Caerleon. York had long been the stronghold of the ruler of the north and even when his power splintered, he is unlikely to have surrendered it to another. Chester had the advantage of being close to an Irish threat and to the northern menace but, though linking into the road network, it was too remote from the English heartland to be ideal. Caerleon was closest of these fortresses to Kent and East Anglia which still posed the greatest military danger to the British. It gave rapid access to the road network and in particular to the Fosse Way which in turn fed into the centre of the web of highways or directly on towards the east coast. It also allowed a rapid response to Irish threats in west Wales or the west country and there was quick access to Chester and the north-west if problems arose there. Though there are cases to be made for other sites for 'Camelot', Caerleon best serves the tactical and practical needs of the warlord of the British. It did not even deprive the local ruler of his capital, for Gwent was ruled from nearby Caerwent.

Year after year Arthur retired at the end of campaigning to the security of his fortress where men and mounts could recover their strength, where weapons, armour and harness could be repaired, where next year's campaigning could be planned. No doubt, he also had to spend part of his winter contending with the politics of the rulers whom he served, for each would have his own agenda and such cross-currents always serve to undermine the soldier in any age. And when spring came it would be into the field again, a constant criss-crossing of Britain to ensure the chain of strongholds continued to pen in the settlers and then seeking out and destroying all attempts to break new ground, and riding into the north or west when those old threats reared their heads again.

A CRUEL AND UNRELENTING PRESSURE

We do not know how long Arthur maintained his incessant pressure on those seeking to settle and on those already there, to the third and fourth generation, or denied the northern and western foes the pickings for which they sniffed. We come tantalisingly close to finding a date for the climax of his campaigns but are denied it by a moment of imprecision on the part of the chronicler. As a result we are left to our own devices to decide whether Arthur waged this brutal and wearing warfare for fifteen or so years or whether it lasted nearer thirty.

But we can reasonably surmise that season after season he took the field with his small army, moving mainly through eastern Britain and more or less living in the saddle. Each attempt by the settlers to break new ground would be met by sudden force, with little likelihood of quarter given. It is unlikely that prisoners were taken, for there was a deep hatred in the British towards men they saw as land thieves and savages. Doubtless, many of the battles left survivors who scrambled back out to sea. But where did they then go? Where could they go? If they sought land on the continent they would fall foul of Clovis' Frankish kingdom. Perhaps returning to their homeland might have been an option but whatever drove them to migrate in the first place must still have been a factor and, since a people does not migrate except under extreme pressure, that was clearly closed to them. Many must have sought refuge among the earliest settlers where they would have been unwelcome.

Natural population growth would by now be placing almost intolerable pressure on the limited land and resources in those original areas and the presence of refugees would take matters to crisis level. Arthur could not break into these areas. Teeming with a hostile population, they would be lethal to cavalry who needed a secure base from which to operate. He lacked the manpower to make a full-scale infantry attack on these formidable warriors who would be defending their homes over ground familiar to them. And there were physical barriers of forest and fen to hinder his operations.

Perhaps he realised that ultimately they must attack him. The kind of pressure he and Ambrosius had created by cramping the settlement areas meant the English must emigrate or starve – or conquer. We know that in another hundred years emigration would be possible because the political circumstances on the continent would actually be conducive – but not now. So the options were starve or conquer. Thus came the crisis.

THE GREAT BATTLE

We know its name: Badon. We know it was a great slaughter. We know it crippled English fighting power for a generation. We know it badly hurt the British. But we do not know where it was or when it was. The time bracket is the closing years of the fifth century and the first fifteen years or so of the sixth century. Some of the evidence suggests a site near modern Swindon, in Wiltshire; other evidence suggests a site near Bath.

The evidence for a site near Swindon derives from suggestions of a concerted onslaught by the English, headed by the King of the South Saxons, Aelle. If the southern English were breaking out northwards, they must, in order to avoid being picked off separately, link up with the Kent men driving west. It was in the interests of the Kent men and the southerners to increase their forces – and thus their chances – by drawing in the East Anglians. The latter would be unlikely to emerge from their fastnesses unless there was some substantial gain for them. Since the Arthurian pressure was probably greatest on the overcrowded east coast lands, the gain for the Anglians would be the breaking of that pressure.

Thus we see a triple break-out from the settled areas towards a single point where they could bring a mass of warriors to bear on the British whose strategy for three generations has been to contain the English and keep them separated.

But there is another element in the choice of this area as the battleground. It is the introduction of another player into the game, one whose presence in the field lends weight to the choice of this area. In the post-Arthurian period a clutch of English kingdoms is to be found, one of them Wessex, the kingdom of the West Saxons, expanding from the area around Winchester. Its traditions attribute its foundation to a warrior called Cerdic and its beginnings can be dated to around the end of the fifth or early sixth century. That is straightforward enough but a complication arises through the name of the founder of the kingdom – it is not a Germanic name (like Aelle, Hengest, etc) but Celtic and possibly Irish. So we are probably looking at either the repudiation of the collective political British leadership by one of its number or a coup by the commander of the local army which contained Germanic mercenaries. If the former, then it would be logical for the local ruler – the said Cerdic – to ensure he was not threatened by his erstwhile colleagues. If the latter, then the usurper – Cerdic – would need to ensure that retribution in the form of Arthur did not come his way.

Logic suggests that whether it was Cerdic the king or Cerdic the usurper, he was a fool to get tied in with the English to destroy British power. But we should never look for logic in the conduct of politics in any age or circumstances. The driving force in most such situations is short-termist and personal. It is for these reasons that we believe it possible that Cerdic threw in his lot with the triple English thrust at Arthur.

An examination of the Roman road network and the old prehistoric trackways shows the likeliest junction of these four forces (Kent men, South Saxons, Anglians and Cerdic) to be just south of Swindon where a prehistoric hillfort dominates the terrain. The presence nearby of a village called Baydon is coincidental.

The East Anglians would travel fastest by using the ancient line of the Ridgeway. The Kent men, needing to evade garrisons designed to keep them and the East Anglians apart, would use the road towards Silchester – itself a node point on the system. For the men of the south a drive up towards Silchester offered an early junction with the Kent men and then on westwards. For Cerdic, the road north from Winchester to Cirencester would bring him to the Kent men and Sussex men just south of Swindon where the Ridgeway – bringing the Anglians – intersects with the Roman roads.

It would have been in English interests to create some kind of distraction, perhaps in collusion with the Picts or even with dissatisfied British elements. Whether Arthur was drawn off, we can never know but the fact that the English got so far into the west suggests he was distracted. Or, knowing this to be the climactic battle of his age, he may simply have let them come deep into his ground, far away from their home areas and onto the killing ground of his choice.

But why would the English and Cerdic converge so far south? Why not seek a more central battleground in terrain where horsemen could operate less easily, such as the forested areas of the midlands? Whether we choose Caerleon or another site for Arthur's headquarters, we can be confident it was deep inside his own territory and sited on or near the road network. The English needed to unite all their forces as rapidly as possible, before he could intervene, and only then bring him to battle. The most certain way of bringing him to battle was to threaten the heartland of British power – the Cotswold/Wiltshire/Dorset area – and menace his own fortress where the families of his soldiers and even his own family were located. Arthur the general might look at this from a strategic point of view and regard his headquarters as expendable if the gain was to get across his enemy's lines of communication and/or get the battleground of his choosing. But Arthur the politician knew his paymasters would sing a different tune if their estates were threatened. And Arthur the leader of men would know the effect on his own soldiers if they were ordered to hazard their own families.

Aelle and his confederates would have weighed up all this for themselves and reckoned a rapid junction and drive into the British heartland, with Caerleon beyond it, would raise the kind of screams in Arthur's ears which must bring him to battle. And they got the battle they wanted.

The evidence in support of the area of Bath is drawn from later written sources and then relies heavily on making a connection between 'Badonis' and Bath, a connection which is by no means certain. If the battle was fought in the area of Bath it suggests the English had been able, or had been allowed, to penetrate deep into British territory (a strong possibility, which has already been discussed). However, it is hard to see what was the English target if the battle was fought around Bath, which could not have had any strategic value; it certainly lacked the fortifications to be Arthur's base. There are two possible explanations for the presence of the English host in that area. Firstly, it had been aiming for another objective (e.g. Caerleon) and had been driven off before being brought to battle near Bath. Or, secondly, the English had come by sea into this area which, again, would be consistent with a thrust at the British heartland and which the latter would be unable to counter. However, there must be serious doubts about the ability of the English to mount an amphibious operation on this scale.

But whether the English and the British came to grips near Bath or near Swindon, the fact remains that the climax of their long struggle was fought out somewhere in the South-West. Doubtless, Arthur had for years planned for this day and now brought to the downs the full fighting force of the British, urging upon their leaders the understanding that this was the crisis of their generation. It was their chance to wipe out the fighting force of the English, their chance to drive these land-wasters from their shores. An aberration by Vortigern had let these savages into Roman territory, with all the consequent dislocation, but now the chance was at hand to reverse it all.

It was a monumental struggle, with terrible loss of life. When it was over the English were in retreat.

PARTITION

But the damage to the British was immense. For the English this had been an all-or-nothing throw of the dice and they had fought with their natural courage allied with sheer desperation. So badly did they maul the Arthurian forces that the pursuit was less than ferocious and when the British did follow up in force they found that they lacked the strength to finish the job. There would be no rooting out of the English settlements, no driving this hated enemy into the sea. The British must face the fact that they now had to live alongside the incomers.

What followed was either a formal agreement which defined the boundaries of the settled areas or simply, and more probably, an unspoken acknowledgement by each side that there was neither peace nor war.

Archaeology indicates that the English withdrew deep into their heartlands, abandoning settlements along their margins. After the butchery at Badon there was probably land to spare. It is clear that a kind of curtain descended between the British and their unwelcome neighbours. There was no social interchange, no trade – nothing. Not even the evangelists, normally the least deterred of men, would cross from British territory in search of converts. We know that plague decimated the British area during this time, brought along the trade routes into the south and west, but it did not touch the English. It appears that not even plague-bearing bacilli would cross the line to go among the English.

PAX ARTHURIANA

Some Welsh traditions refer to Arthur as 'emperor'. This may simply be the hyperbole of legend but it may also reflect the post-Roman soldiers of Britain recalling their heritage. For the word emperor derives from the salute given to the victorious commander by the legion – imperator.

This perhaps was the victory cry on the corpse-strewn flanks of the hills around Badon. But the Welsh sources may more simply reflect the aura of the man who dominated the last decades of Roman Britain. It is clear there was a last period of calm and peace for the Romano-British. Without external threat to disturb them, the rulers of Britain enjoyed their domains and governed their subjects in the way Rome had taught.

No political system is unflawed and there is no such thing as a truly golden age – the lustre is usually seen through hindsight. So there were abuses and injustices amidst all this but the overlapping generation and particularly its successor recalled it as a time which compared more than favourably with what followed.

Arthur's army would have been disbanded after Badon: the rulers had borne the burden for long enough and could now reasonably say the threat was broken. Perhaps he retained a small force which could be a cadre in the event of unforeseen hostilities, but he no longer ranged Britain in force, cowing enemy and friend alike. No doubt his battle-weary and ageing bones relished this. But his prestige was such that his presence alone would impose checks on those who thought to disrupt the peace he had achieved. Besides, most of those rulers were men who had fought and suffered alongside him during the long years of war and they were for the most part wise and sensible enough to recognise the magnitude of their achievement. They were unlikely to prejudice it. So this system of personalised checks and balances gave to Roman Britain a last flowering after almost a century of war and dislocation. But such times usually contain the seeds of their own decay.

DEATH

Kings and princes die. Rarely in history does a capable heir succeed a capable parent, for such is the principal defect of the hereditary system. The men who fought alongside Arthur died and their heirs came into their own. Many were young men grown weary of listening to old men's tales of how they went with great Arthur against the tribesmen and destroyed them. Who were these tribesmen? Savages, cowering in their settlement areas and no threat to anyone. These new rulers had armies and they had ambitions. Why should they not expand their inheritance? Why should they not grow and grow until they were a great ruler in their own right?

Well, one reason was that greying old dog of war who prowled around to ensure they lived in amity, preserving this peace he droned on about and which seemed to have been his whole life. Worse for them was the prospect that he may have had a successor in place. We cannot be sure about this but it is possible Arthur intended another warlord to be available amongst the British after he was dead or retired. He perhaps intended the creation of an institution by which to prevent a recurrence of the crisis which had been ended at Badon. If he did, the new generation was having none of it. And if he had no such intention, then their strike against him was simply to remove the restraining hand.

Of the events themselves we know nothing. We do know that Arthur was killed in battle at Camlann where the enemy was either his own people or a non-English foe such as the Picts. The site of Camlann is unknown and even more difficult to guess at than Badon. The suggested sites range from Cornwall to Cumbria. But killed Arthur was and within a couple of decades everything he achieved was wrecked.

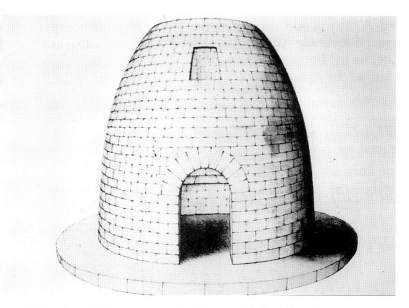

1 Early print of a Roman construction known as 'Arthur's Oven', near Stenhousemuir in Stirlingshire (since destroyed)

2 Arthur's Seat, Edinburgh – possible site of Nennius's 'Battle of Agned'

3 Little Solsbury Hillfort, possible site of the Battle of Badon

4 Glastonbury Tor, legendary site of the abduction of Guinevere

5 Marduk and the captured Winlogee (Guinevere) from the Modena Archivolt, carving Norman with Breton names, about 1110

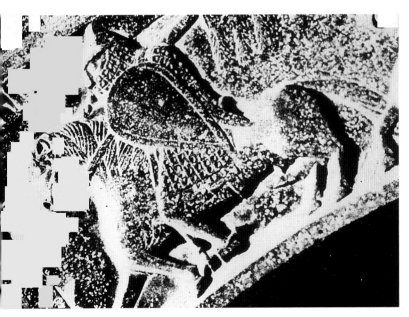

6 Galviginus (Gawain) rides to rescue Winlogee (Guinevere) on the Modena Archivolt, carved by Normans with Breton names about 1110

7 Portchester Castle (Hampshire), possible site of the Battle of Llongborth

8 Caerlaverock Castle (Dumfriesshire) – 'The Fort of the Lark' connected in Welsh legend with Merlin

9 Lady Charlotte Guest's illustration for the tale of 'Culhwych and Olwen' from *The Mabinogion*

10 Tintagel Castle and Merlin's Cave

11 Tintagel Castle

12 Tintagel Castle showing the early defensive ditch to the left

13 Remains of a tenth-century church on the plateau above Tintagel Castle

14 Early Christian burial mound, Tintagel Churchyard

15 Glastonbury Abbey: the nave and the old monks' cemetery, from which the bones of Arthur were allegedly exhumed

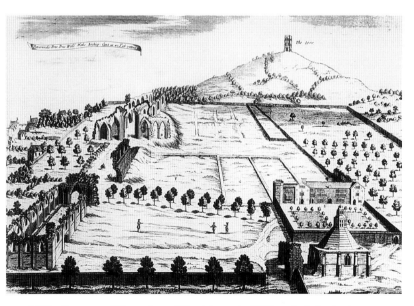

16 'The Prospect of Glastonbury Abbey' drawn by William Stukeley in the eighteenth century

17 Lancelot as a baby and the Lady of the Lake

18 Lancelot as 'The Knight of the Cart' in Chretien's romance

19 Lancelot hastening to the Dolorous Garde in the French Vulgate Cycle

20 Lancelot and his knights leaving Joyous Garde in the French Vulgate Cycle

21 A Celtic Magic Cauldron illustrated by Lady Charlotte Guest in her edition of
The Mabinogion

22 Galahad arrives at Arthur's Court. From a French thirteenth-century
manuscript

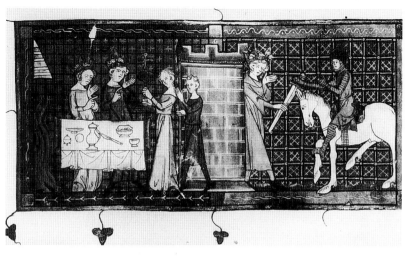

23 Perceval arrives at the Grail Castle. From a French thirteenth-century manuscript

24 Bamburgh Castle, Northumberland, possible site of Lancelot's Castle 'Joyous Garde' according to Sir Thomas Malory. The Celtic name for the site was 'Din Guayrdi'

THE LADY OF THE LAKE
TELLETH ARTHVR OF THE
SWORD EXCALIBVR

25 'The Lady of the Lake telleth Arthur of the Sword Excalibur.' *Illustration by Aubrey Beardsley for Malory's* Le Morte D'Arthur, 1885

26 Guinevere. *Drawing by William Morris*

27 Cadbury Castle from the north. *Drawing by William Stukeley,* 1723

28 Rampart of Cadbury Castle (Somerset). Possible Arthurian stronghold

3 After the Darkness

ENGLISH DAWN

Locked within their settlement areas, the English numbers began to grow again but the scars left by that long and bloody struggle with the Arthurian British continued to hurt. The renewed population pressure did not lead to new attempts to break out – on the contrary, there is evidence to show there was a kind of reverse migration to the continent. Settlers from England were used by the Frankish kings to strengthen their grip on their German territories.

There is a school of opinion which believes that, far from being penned within their settlement areas and sending their surplus population overseas, the English were encroaching on the British-held areas in the east and, piece by piece, were taking control of territories along their common border. However, this opinion relies heavily on an interpretation of a contemporary written source which is not borne out by archaeology.

What archaeology and written sources do point towards is the eventual realisation by the English that what they thought was a barrier was in fact an open door. They probably pushed on it more in hope than in anticipation and found this time there was no bar. The kings who should have been the doorkeepers, the custodians of the Arthurian legacy, were too busy fighting among themselves to notice the renewal of the old danger. Now there was no warlord to jerk them to their senses; no longer were the vigilant eyes directed at the fringes of the settled areas to warn of probing raids. Nor, any longer, did the English need to concert their efforts because now there was no single hand to bring down the full fighting strength of the British.

Out of the kingdoms of Kent, of Sussex and of Wessex came warbands to conquer new lands. Out of East Anglia came settlers to break new ground. In the north new settlements were gouged where none dared try before. The British response was piecemeal and ineffectual and in a generation eastern Britain had become England.

CELTIC TWILIGHT

A brave attempt was made in the north to stem this tide and came within a whisker of rooting out the new English settlements but the British king was murdered by his own kind even as he stood to deliver the killing blow. With him died the last real chance of uprooting the northern English; now the British were on the defensive.

Another part of the British response was migration. Thousands crossed to Brittany, taking with them the bright new memory of a warrior leader who had crushed an enemy they equated with the forces of darkness. That memory would be burnished and embellished until it became a legend from which the medieval world would create the epitome of chivalry.

The kinfolk the migrants left behind became foreigners in their own country (the word 'Welsh' is derived from the Early English word for foreigner). During the earliest part of the English settlement the native British fled, for their attackers had a justifiable reputation for savagery. But during the second phase of the conquest there was, apart from the one last spasm mentioned above, less migration. The native British were conquered and reduced to slavery or (in Wessex) to second-class freemen. With time they became indistinguishable from the conquerors; their language vanished to the extent that only in a few areas did it survive through place names.

Only in the far west and in Wales, and for a while in what is now south west Scotland, did the British and their language cling to a separate identity. Those were the very areas where Romanity had lain thinnest and so they were not the places where it could find a new form and live on. But the irony is that it is here, where resistance to Rome had been strongest, that the memory was preserved of the man whose life had been devoted to fighting to maintain that now-lost Romano-British way of life. Among those people Arthur became what they most admired: the quintessential warrior chieftain and in that form he passed on into their folklore. Because Rome had ceased to matter to those who maintained the Arthurian flame, the very reason for his fame became forgotten.

It is one of history's quirks that the reality which spawned the legend has been erased. This is where lies the fascination: for history as we construct it can be far less absorbing than the illusion we enjoy.

PART II

THE ARTHURIAN LEGENDS
FRAN AND GEOFF DOEL

'How King Marke found Sir Tristram.' *Drawing by Aubrey Beardsley*

Introduction

The quest for the historical Arthur is both exciting and enriching. But when we leave the factual world of historian and archaeologist for the more shadowy realm of legend and culture, then paradoxically the figure of Arthur achieves a greater clarity and archetypal significance as it is adapted and remoulded for successive cultures by a series of outstanding writers. These cultural layers which shape the Arthurian legend equate to archaeological layers denoting reuse of a site by successive cultures. And, as with an archaeological record, some knowledge of the cultures is needed to explain the context and significance. In the opinion of the Greek philosopher Aristotle:

> Poetry is something more philosophical and more worthy of serious attention than history; for while poetry is concerned with universal truths, history treats of particular facts.
> (*On the Art of Poetry, Ch. 9*)

Aristotle's comment can be seen as a corrective to those many historians who have believed a study of Arthur to be irrelevant as his existence cannot be proved. Whether or not Arthur existed (and strong circumstantial evidence suggests he did), the power, durability and adaptability of his legends suggest that 'universal truths' may be discovered by an exploration of the legends. In this section of the book we intend to explore Arthur's shifting mythical and cultural significance through literature – how the legends both influence and reflect cultural change in the countries and societies through which they pass. From the earliest Welsh sources with their overtones of Celtic mythology to John Arden's anti-imperialist play *The Island of the Mighty* in the 1970s and Marion Bradley's feminist novel *The Mists of Avalon* in the 1980s, the legends have shown amazing vitality, adaptability and flexibility in successive literary treatments in different countries, cultures and languages, by clerics and laymen, by poets, novelists and dramatists. Successive cultures recreated Arthur and his 'knights' in their own image, though some continuity in the legends was achieved through their very potency and memorability.

Legendary allusions abound. Arthur, as leader, warrior, hero, lover and British champion against the invading Anglo-Saxons, is a vital cultural figure in early Celtic literature and lore. By the twelfth century he has become a pan-European figure, a dominant motif in literary and artistic culture, a focal point for the cults of chivalry and courtly love and for esoteric mysteries such as the Holy Grail. Already, in the twelfth century, historians such as William of Malmesbury, Caradoc of Llancarfon and Gerald of Wales are trying to disentangle fact from fiction.

The potency of the Arthurian legends may reflect the remarkable achievements of the historical Arthur. But undoubtedly a factor in their cultural power and adaptability was that from the earliest stages the mythos of Arthur absorbed aspects of Celtic religion and deification, such as the mysterious birth, the sword in the stone, the water deities (ladies of the lake), the cauldron of immortality and the Other World and, most importantly, an element found in many religions, the Second Coming. The messianic nature of this Celtic mythical Arthur made him a political force to be reckoned with wherever Celtic peoples were involved, right up to the Tudor myth exploited by Henry Tudor and his son, Henry the Eighth, who employed the antiquarian John Leland to disprove Polydore Vergil's assertion that Arthur was an unhistorical myth.

The Arthurian legendary material has attracted many of the great writers of European civilisation – Taliesin, Geoffrey of Monmouth, Wace, Chretien De Troyes, Gottfried von Strassburg, Wolfram von Eschenbach, Geoffrey Chaucer, the anonymous 'Gawain' poet, Sir Thomas Malory, Edmund Spenser, Alfred Tennyson, Thomas Hardy, T. S. Eliot, John Arden. The early Arthurian folklore is found, as one would expect, in the Celtic areas of Wales, Cornwall, Britanny and to a lesser extent Cumbria and parts of Scotland. His entrance into English culture is via the aristocratic and educated and English folklore (apart from Cornish) tends to develop later (with the interesting exception of South Cadbury) and to be associated with Arthurian literature, particularly the influential Tennyson and Malory. It is perhaps not until Tennyson's enormously popular *Idylls of the King* that Arthur becomes a British hero for both English and Celtic peoples of all classes. This section of the book is the story of this fascinating development.

4 The Medieval Welsh Sources

If Arthur is thought of historically as a late Romano-British leader based in the West of Britain fighting against the Anglo-Saxons and their Pictish and Irish allies, we should expect the earliest legends, stories, poems and place names associated with him to emerge in the post-Roman Celtic cultures which were the legacy of the collapse of Roman Britain. For the Anglo-Saxons, who fought against Arthur, would not have been interested in preserving his name or deeds. No Anglo-Saxon reference to the British victory at Mount Badon survives, though there is a reference to a 'second' Battle of Badon (which the Anglo-Saxons won) in the Welsh Annals, a mid-tenth-century copy of monastic Easter tables. The battle is significantly sited in the west of England.

However, the surviving Celts in the west of Britain would be expected to preserve in their oral culture traditions of a man who held the Germanic barbarians at bay in a way unparalleled in the rest of Europe. The Celtic church had a monopoly of literacy and some Arthurian material (presumably originally from oral sources) survives in monkish chronicles and saints' lives written in Latin. The development of written Celtic languages led to the writing down of many poems and stories about Arthur, most of which probably originated in oral tradition.

THE CHRONICLES

Two monkish chroniclers (writing in Latin) are of particular interest. St Gildas gives a nearly contemporary reference to the great British victory at Mount Badon which he tells us was fought in the year of his birth, 'forty-four years' ago. Scholars have dated his *The Ruin of Britain* to the 540s (one of the dating factors is that Maelgwn of Gwynedd and Arthur's successor Constantine were apparently still alive when the book was written). Unfortunately Gildas does not mention Arthur in his book, which is religious in impetus, but he does mention Arthur's predecessor, Ambrosius, and his successor Constantine – a King of Dumnonia (Devon, Cornwall and part of Somerset). Gildas's references to Ambrosius and Constantine are sufficient to place their existence beyond doubt and to show that

Arthur is at least framed between historical rulers who are featured in the same legendary material. Gildas's reference to the Battle of Mount Badon ('*Badonici montis*') is generally accepted as proof of that event.

The second chronicler, Nennius, writes in the early ninth century and is acutely aware both of his own Welsh Bardic tradition and earlier chroniclers such as Gildas and Bede. Nennius's aims are creditably historical, as outlined in a preface found in the later manuscripts of the selection of documents which scholars call *Select Documents of Early British History*:

> I, Nennius, disciple of the saintly Elbodugus [probably Elfodd, Bishop of Bangor in place by 768, died *c.*811], have written down some excerpts that the ignorance of the British cast out; for the scholars of the Island of Britain had no written ability to set down information in books. I have therefore grouped together all that I could find – from the Annals of the Romans, the Chronicles of the Holy Fathers, the writings of the Irish and the English, and the tradition of our elders. ★

Nennius lists considerable material about Vortigern. There are two references to Ambrosius, one citing him as an important ruler of the British and the other involving legendary material about the death of Vortigern (Geoffrey of Monmouth replaces Ambrosius by Merlin in his account). Nennius does not include Gildas's reference to Ambrosius initiating and leading the fight back against the Saxons culminating in Badon. But he does include a list of Arthur's battles and specifically places Arthur as the victor at Badon. It is the first account of Arthur's military career which we have:

> At that time the English multiplied their numbers and expanded in Britain. After the death of Hengest, his son Octha came down from the north of Britain to the kingdom of Kent, and from him are sprung the kings of Kent. Then Arthur fought against them in those days, together with the kings of the British; but he was their '*dux bellorum*' [leader in battle].
>
> The first battle was at the mouth of the river which is called Glein. The second, the third, the fourth and the fifth were upon another river, which

★N.J. Higham has produced a comprehensive analysis of 'Nennius', giving the political, historical and cultural context (see Higham, *King Arthur: Myth-Making and History*, pp.119-166)

is called Dubglas and is in the region of Linnuis. The sixth battle was upon the river which is called Bassas. The seventh battle was in the wood of Celidon, it is Cat Coit Celidon. The eighth battle was in the castle Guinnion in which Arthur carried the image of St Mary, the ever-virgin upon his shoulders, and the pagans were put to flight on that day, and there was a great slaughter of them, through the virtue of Our Lord Jesus Christ and the virtue of St Mary the Virgin, his mother. The ninth battle was fought in the City of the Legion. The tenth battle was fought on the bank of the river which is called Tribruit. The eleventh battle was on the mountain which is called Agned. The twelfth battle was on Mount Badon, wherein fell nine hundred and sixty men in one day at a single charge of Arthur; and no one laid them low save he alone, and he was victorious in all his campaigns.

This extract suggests that Arthur was a war leader rather than a king and that he was (as we would expect) a Christian. Those battle sites which can might be identified are far-flung; four in the Lincoln area (Lindsey) where archaeological work on the gateway to the Roman fort suggests considerable conflict (presumably between the British and Anglo-Saxons) at this period. Later literary and legendary sources suggest that the Scottish sites reflect Pictish adversaries, but some historians suggest warfare against early Irish settlers from the Argyll area or successor groupings of the Novantae/Selgovae/Votadini. The location of the 'City of the Legion' (either Caerleon or Chester) certainly suggests war against the Irish, although Christopher Gidlow in *The Reign of Arthur* suggests the Saxons.

Nennius also refers to Arthurian folklore in his section on 'The Wonders of Britain'. He mentions a stone on a cairn with a footprint of Arthur's dog (Carn Cafal near Builth) and the tomb near a spring of Arthur's son Amr in Ergyng, with the tradition that Arthur killed and buried his son. Nennius's third 'wonder' is:

The Hot Lake, where the Baths of Badon are, which is in the country of the Hwicce and is surrounded by a wall, made of brick and stone, and men may go there to bathe at any time, and every man can have the kind of bath he wishes. If he wishes he can have a cold bath, and if he wants a hot bath, it will be hot.

Nennius's Latin word for both the battle site and the hot springs (which are clearly the springs at Bath – which lay in the territory of the Hwicce) is *Badonis* (similar to Gildas's *'Badonici montis'*). This clearly points to Bath as the site for the Battle of Badon (perhaps Little Solsbury hillfort). Geoffrey of Monmouth gives Bath as the site in his *History of the Kings of Britain* (1136). However most historians find this site uncomfortably far west, though it is strategically placed near the Fosse Way. It is worth pointing out that few battles are fought at sites where later military tacticians would ideally have placed them!

Nennius does not refer to Arthur's death, but the Welsh Annals (whose specific items are difficult to date) mention both the Battle of Badon and, twenty-one years later, Arthur's death at the Battle of Camlann: 'The battle of Camlann, in which Arthur and Medraut perished.'

The Welsh Annals are in Latin, but the Welsh word for battle, 'Gueith', is used for Camlann, presumably indicating a Welsh source. Geoffrey of Monmouth, using 'a certain very ancient book written in the British language' as one of his sources, places the site of this battle on the River Camel in Cornwall and says:

> Arthur himself, our renowned King, was mortally wounded and was carried off to the Isle of Avalon, so that his wounds might be attended to. He handed the crown of Britain over to his cousin Constantine, the son of Cador Duke of Cornwall: this in the year 542 after our Lord's Incarnation.

Geoffrey (supported by Welsh poetic tradition where Mordred is called Medraut) specifies that Camlann is a civil war between Arthur and his nephew Mordred, 'the accursed traitor', who has usurped Arthur's realm, allied with the Saxons and committed adultery with his queen Guinevere. Constantine is historical, one of the five kings of western Britain mentioned by Gildas and still alive when Gildas wrote about 540.

So Welsh chronicle traditions imply that Arthur was struck down by that typically Celtic phenomenon of civil war, but that Saxon troops were involved. Following the Gildas dating for Badon plus the Welsh Annals gap of twenty-one years between the Battles of Badon and Camlann, this puts Arthur's death at about 520. This is many years before the Saxons resumed their westward settlement, according to the archaeological evidence so far, and would suggest that the battle in which Arthur died may not have had immediate national repercussions. However, both the cross-dating evidence for the Annals and Geoffrey of Monmouth suggest a later date for Camlann. This in turn implies a later date for Badon, which would raise other problems of interpretation. The difficulties in reconciling these two schemes of dating is a major obstacle to understanding Arthur's historical role.

THE LIVES OF SAINTS

Further Latin references to Arthur survive in Welsh Saints' Lives, written by monks. These are not very complimentary and refer to Arthur as '*tyrannus*'. The Chambers Dictionary definition of 'tyrant' points out that this was 'in the original Greek sense, an absolute ruler, or one whose power has not been constitutionally arrived at'. This is probably the intended meaning in the Saints' Lives and would fit in with our perceived view of the historical Arthur as a military ruler, for whom one of these saints, St Illtud, apparently fought in his younger days. Interestingly. *The Life of St Gildas* refers to Arthur as '*rex rebelliosus*' (rebellious king). This suggests a scenario of an Arthur who achieved power, prestige and land by military prowess, (a comparison might be the Duke of Wellington in the early nineteenth century) rather than by royal lineage. The controversy over Arthur's origins and birth in the legends and early literary accounts lend some support to this idea.

The Saints' Lives also invariably show the particular saint in question outwitting and/or dominating the ruler Arthur, though not seeking to overthrow or permanently damage him. These stories may be evidence that Arthur was an important folklore figure and that the saints could achieve prestige by outwitting him, but they may reflect a tradition of hostility between Arthur and the Church. Arthur and the Church are never shown as being on different sides (after all he was the Church's protector against the heathen Saxons and perhaps in Wales against the inroads of the Irish), but there are hints about disputes over money and goods, which may be a memory of some levy on the Church for campaigns, and over power control, always a problem between Church and secular ruler in the middle ages.

Five Saints' Lives from the major hagiographic centre at Llancarfan in Glamorgan mention Arthur. All the saints concerned are approximately contemporary with Arthur, but their *Lives* are written down in the late eleventh or twelfth centuries. The earliest is probably *The Life of St Cadoc*, which is attributed to Lifri in the late eleventh century. There are two separate stories about Arthur in this '*Life*', separated by a rather large time gap. In the first episode, Cadoc's future mother Gwladys elopes with the

King of Glamorgan and they come across Arthur playing dice with his favourite followers in the Welsh tradition – Cai and Bedwyr (later known as Kay and Bedivere). Arthur takes a fancy to Gwladys, but is restrained by his followers who remind him of their duty to help those in distress:

> Behold, three noble heroes, Arthur and his two companions, Cai and Bedwyr, were sitting on a hilltop, playing dice. When they saw the king and the girl, Arthur's heart was filled with desire. Full of bad thoughts, he said to his companions: 'I am burning with desire for the maiden whom that warrior is carrying on his horse.' But they answered: 'You must not do anything so unlawful; we are supposed to help those in distress and need. Let us help these people who need succour.' Arthur replied: 'Very well, if you would rather help him than secure the maiden for me, go and ask on whose land they are fighting.'

Persuaded by his friends, Arthur supports the marriage of Gwladys to the King of Glamorgan against the wishes of Gwladys' father, King Brychan. Although not an entirely flattering portrait, this story hints at Arthur's importance and is an interesting pre-French example of a kind of embryonic knightly code of helping those in distress – a fascinating aspect of Arthurian tradition. And there is humour in Arthur being reminded by his companions of how he is supposed to act. In this story Arthur behaves more like a Welsh tribal ruler than the late Romano-British war leader of the chronicles or the later absolute monarch in the French stories.

Many years later in the story, Gwladys's son, Cadoc, by then Abbot of Llancarfon, clashes with Arthur by giving sanctuary to 'a certain Ligessauc, who was a very brave leader of the Britons', but had killed three of the warriors of Arthur ('the most famous king of Britain'). Ligessauc is hiding in the monastery of Cadoc (who 'has no fear of Arthur') for seven years and Arthur protests that sanctuary cannot exist for so long. The case is adjudicated on the banks of the River Usk and Arthur is awarded compensation of a hundred cows because Cadoc has exceeded his rights. As the cattle are driven across the river by Arthur, Cei and Bedwyr, they change into bundles of fern. Overcome by this demonstration of supernatural power, Arthur acknowledges Cadoc's right to give sanctuary for seven years, seven months and seven days.

The Celtic shape-shifting magic in this story is typical of early Welsh tales, but it may be that some legal dispute between the Church and a secular ruler or war leader lies behind this tale; or it may simply be an ecclesiastical ploy to bolster St Cadoc's reputation and to give a legal basis for monastic claims for sanctuary. Already Arthur's reputation is undergoing cultural distortion to help the needs and propaganda of the Church.

In *The Life of Saint Carannog*, the saint floats his altar across the Severn Estuary into the country of Dindraithov (modern Dunster), ruled by Cato and Arthur. The saint is seeking his altar and Arthur is looking for a serpent who is ravaging the country. They do a deal: Carannog controls the serpent and Arthur restores the altar, which he has been using as a table and he and Cadwy grant land to the saint, on which he builds a church and a monastery.

Once again power control, acquisition of church property and an uneasy 'deal' are the main features of the story. Cato (also known as Cadwy and Cador) features prominently in Arthurian literature and legend and is the father of the historical Constantine, who (in legend) succeeds Arthur and is ruler of Dumnonia, an independent kingdom in the southwest. So Cato would presumably be the legal ruler at Dunster and the fact that Arthur is shown as a co-ruler indicates his military prestige and importance in the area.

In *The Life of St Padarn*, the *tyrannus* Arthur is again collecting Church valuables – on this occasion he enters Padarn's cell and tries to take a tunic and, on the saint's instruction, is swallowed up to the chin by the earth and only released after apologising:

> ... a *tyrannus* from foreign lands ... greedily demanded bishop Paternus' vestment. Paternus responded: 'This vestment was not intended to be worn by ungodly men, but for priests.' Arthur left the monastery very angry and returned to try to take the tunic by force ... cursing and swearing and stamping the ground. Paternus commanded: 'Let the earth swallow him.' The earth immediately opened and swallowed Arthur up to the chin ... He begged forgiveness; the earth vomited him up ... the saint forgave him.

Once again Arthur is humbled by a saint invoking divine or supernatural aid to prove his superiority. But underlying this story could there be a tradition of Arthur levying money and goods for his campaigns against the Saxons or Irish?

The Life of St Illtud, who was a Breton, says that the saint was a cousin of Arthur and originally one of his soldiers:

> Illtud heard of the magnificence of King Arthur and longed to visit the court
> of so great a conqueror ...When he arrived he saw a multitude of soldiers ...
> and he was given a commission appropriate to his military ambition. When
> he had achieved the honours he sought, he left the court highly respected
> and visited Poulentus, king of Glamorgan, who employed him because he
> was a royal soldier ... preferring him to all his own military companions ...
> and appointed him as his *magister militum* [commander-in-chief].

The possibility that St Illtud had once been a soldier fighting for
Arthur should be taken seriously as this tradition seems to be more than
an ecclesiastical piece of propaganda. And the idea of Breton support for
the Ambrosian and Arthurian campaign against the Saxons finds support
in Geoffrey of Monmouth and from modern historians and, given the
common enemy and common religious and racial bond, seems highly
likely. The story also hints at the power of Arthur's recommendation of
military personnel to the local kings.

Caradoc of Llancarfan's *Life of St Gildas*, written in about 1130, has several
Arthurian references. This is that same Gildas who wrote *The Ruin of Britain*
in the sixth century. According to Caradoc, Gildas was one of twenty-four
sons of Nau, king of Scotia. Gildas' brethren (presumably they were Picts)
did not accept Arthur's authority, and Arthur killed the eldest, Hueil:

> St Gildas was the contemporary of Arthur, the king of the whole of Britain,
> whom he loved exceedingly, and whom he always desired to obey. Neverthe-
> less his twenty-three brothers constantly rose up against the aforementioned
> rebellious king, refusing to own him as their lord; but they often routed and
> drove him out from forest and the battlefield. Hueil, the elder brother, an ac-
> tive warrior and most distinguished soldier, submitted to no king, not even
> to Arthur. He used to harass the latter, and to provoke the greatest anger
> between them both. He would often swoop down from Scotland, set up
> conflagrations, and carry off spoils with victory and renown. In consequence,
> the king of all Britain, on hearing that the high-spirited youth had done such
> things...pursued the victorious and excellent youth, who, as the inhabitants
> used to assert and hope, was destined to become king. In hostile pursuit and
> council of war held in the island of Minau, he killed the young plunderer.
> ... When King Arthur and the chief bishops and abbots of all Britain heard
> of the arrival of Gildas the Wise, large numbers from among the clergy and

people gathered together to reconcile Arthur for the above-mentioned murder. But Gildas ... was courteous to his enemy, kissed him as he prayed for forgiveness, and with a most tender heart blessed him ... King Arthur, in grief and tears, accepted the penance imposed by the bishops who were present, and led an amended course, as far as he could, until the close of his life. (Translation by Hugh Williams in *Two Lives of St Gildas,* Llanerch)

Arthur's and Gildas's life spans almost certainly did overlap, (since Gildas puts the date of Badon in the year of his own birth), but Arthur may well have died before Gildas became famous and the meeting and penance could be a propaganda exercise. Not so the Pictish campaigns, however, which are mentioned by other chroniclers. The possibility that Arthur killed one of Gildas' relatives is intriguing given the suggestions by some historians that Gildas omitted Arthur's name and share of the Mount Badon triumph over the Saxons in his book *The Ruin of Britain* because of personal animosity.

Caradoc also gives an early account of the popular and enduring theme of the abduction of Guinevere:

... He [Gildas] left the island [the Orcades], embarked on board a small ship, and ... put in at Glastonia, at the time when king Melvas was reigning in the summer country. He was received with much welcome by the abbot of Glastonia, and taught the brethren and the scattered people, sowing the precious seed of the heavenly doctrine. It was there that he wrote the history of the kings of Britain ... It [Glastonbury] was besieged by the tyrant Arthur with a countless multitude on account of his wife Gwenhwyfar, whom the aforesaid wicked king had violated and carried off, and brought there for protection, owing to the asylum afforded by the invulnerable position due to the fortifications of thickets of reed, river, and marsh. The rebellious king had searched for the queen throughout the course of one year, and at last heard that she remained there. Thereupon he roused the armies of the whole of Cornubia and Dibneria; war was prepared between the enemies.

When he saw this, the abbot of Glastonia, attended by the clergy and Gildas the Wise, stepped in between the contending armies, and in a peaceable manner advised his king, Melvas, to restore the ravished lady. Accordingly, she who was to be restored was restored in peace and good will. When these things were done, the two kings gave to the abbot a gift of many domains; and they came to visit the temple of St Mary and to pray, while the abbot confirmed the beloved brotherhood in return for the peace they enjoyed and the benefits which they had conferred, and were more abundantly about to confer. Then the kings returned reconciled, promising reverently to obey the most venerable abbot of Glastonia, and never to violate the most sacred place nor even the districts adjoining the chief's seat.

(Translation by Hugh Williams in *Two Lives of Gildas,* Llanerch)

The ravishing and abduction of Arthur's queen is recounted in Welsh poetry, in French poetry and prose and depicted in a Norman carving on an archivolt at Modena cathedral of about 1110, with Breton names carved under the characters. Her pre-Lancelot abductors mostly have names beginning with 'M' – Medraut in the Welsh, Modred in Geoffrey of Monmouth's Latin, Marduk on the Modena Archivolt and Melegaunt in the French; and in Caradoc's version it is Melvas, King of the Summer Country, who has abducted her to Glastonbury Tor. This is the earliest association of Arthur and Glastonbury and given the Tor's Otherworld traditions, it is interesting that in Chretien De Troyes's French version later in the same century, Guinevere is specifically taken to the Otherworld. Although Arthur's queen may well have been abducted (causing the Battle of Camlann according to Welsh tradition) we also seem here to be in the presence of an archetypal myth – a Celtic parallel to the abduction of Persephone. And it is significant that Arthur searches for a year for his queen – suggesting a seasonal-cyclical motif. This is one of many examples of Arthurian material acquiring or reinforcing European mythological material.

Arthur's armed assistance comes from the western kingdom of Dumnonia, which essentially consists of Cornwall and Devon. We have seen how the Cornovii were probably moved into the western part of the area by Vortigern. Many of the legendary texts we shall be considering show associations between Arthur and Dumnonia. This may reflect the fact that he originated in this area and retained strong family and territorial links. We have already seen that the *Life of St Carannog* shows Arthur ruling Dunster jointly with 'Cato'. Cato is the Roman name of Cadwy or Cador, son of Geraint (whom Arthur assisted in battle according to the Welsh poem *The Elegy for Geraint* to be considered in the next section) and father of the historical Constantine mentioned by Gildas and Arthur's successor, according to Geoffrey of Monmouth, whose Duke Cador is Arthur's right-hand man and Duke of Cornwall.

The intervention of the Abbot of Glastonbury seems to come from one of the many forged claims by the Abbey of Glastonbury to provide proof for claims to certain lands and rights and to privileges and status through seniority of antiquity. This story of ecclesiastical intervention may survive right through to Malory where the Pope intervenes to force the return of Arthur's queen.

The Arthurian material in the Saints' Lives, although written down hundreds of years after Arthur's death, would seem to reflect early Welsh traditions, stories and lore about Arthur, fashioned to accommodate the merit and prestige of the particular saints, who were his contemporaries. Whilst confirming, as we would expect, that Arthur was a Christian and was to a certain extent protecting the church, the Saints' Lives hint at a certain discord between Arthur and the Church over jurisdiction, possessions and authority. Perhaps, however, these stories are too rooted in folklore to be credible as historical evidence, or perhaps the antipathy of some of the writers towards Arthur is racial, cultural or religious, or perhaps they are simply building up the reputation of their saints by showing them as getting the better of the renowned Arthur. Could it just be, however, that we have folk memories of a kind of protection money or levy which caused resentment within the Celtic Church?

There are also some Breton Saints' Lives which refer to Arthur. *The Life of St Goueznou* (*c.*1019) says that the arrogance of the Saxon settlers in Britain 'was subsequently checked for a while by the great Arthur, king of the Britons, so that they were largely restrained and forced to serve'. *The Life of Saint Euflamm* (twelfth century) gives further evidence of Arthur as a legendary dragon-slayer.

WELSH ARTHURIAN POETRY

The Arthurian material incorporated in Welsh chronicles and Saints' Lives in Latin is paralleled by numerous Arthurian references, stories and anecdotes in early Welsh poetry and prose. Arthur was clearly the dominant legendary and mythical force in Wales throughout the middle ages, and the Welsh gloried in him as a symbol of victory against the Saxon oppressor. The transmutation of Arthurian legendary material is an important reflector of cultural change in medieval Wales, particularly in the inter-relationship with the development of the French Arthurian romances in the twelfth and thirteenth centuries.

Most of the Arthurian literary references survive in manuscript form in *The Four Ancient Books of Welsh Poetry* – *The Book of Taliesin*; *The Book of Aneirin; The Black Book of Carmarthen* and *The Red Book of Hergest*; plus a prose collection in *The White Book of Rhydderch*. Scholars date these manuscripts from the end of the twelfth century to the end of the fourteenth century and detect traces of Old Welsh forms in a number of the poems which might place them back as far as the ninth century in their earliest written form, with the distinct possibility of oral currency before that. So, although the Arthurian poems cannot be proved to be early enough to give a contemporary account of Arthur, they do give us a strong insight into the Welsh legendary material prior to Geoffrey of Monmouth's popularisation of Arthur in the early twelfth century and prior to the French romances.

The Welsh poetic material is the residue of the cultural traditions of the whole of the Celtic peoples in Britain and several of the 'Welsh' bards come from areas remote from the present day country of Wales. Extensive scholarship needs to be done on the development of Celtic poetry from oral tradition to written forms before clear judgement can be made of the full significance of the Welsh Arthurian poetic corpus. But there are tantalising possibilities. Could the poem *Y Gododdin*, attributed to Aneirin, in which the poet claimed to be present at the Battle of Catraeth (about 601 AD) against the Saxons and to have witnessed the bravery of one of his comrades, Gwawrddur, who '*gochone brein du ar uur caer ceni bei ef Arthur*' (glutted black ravens on the wall of the fort although he was not Arthur) be traceable in some form back to a composition of that famous bard in the oral tradition? Celtic bards did compose such heroic elegies – many scholars think that genuine poems by Taliesin about his chief Urien survive in the same collections, even though the linguistic indications in Aneirin's and Taliesin's poems suggest tenth century written forms. If this is a poem by Aneirin, it is our earliest reference to Arthur and portrays him as an heroic yardstick against whom other heroes can be measured.

The poem also refers to cavalry being used against the Saxons, which fits in with historical theories about the Romano-British/Celtic fightback against the Saxons led by Ambrosius being effected partly through the use of cavalry. There are contemporary references to Gallic cavalry successes against Germanic foot-soldiers in the Arthurian period.

Traditions of Arthur's mounted knights succouring those in distress occur in Welsh pre-romance works and might have some basis in reality. Arthurian cavalry traditions are also found in a remarkably interesting poem known as 'The Elegy for Gereint', found in two manuscripts

— *The Black Book of Carmarthen* and *The Red Book of Hergest* — which
recounts a rare Arthurian defeat:

Before Geraint who ravaged the foe
I saw horses, white with red feet,
And after the shouting a bitter grave.

Before Geraint, who plundered the foe,
I saw horses, their feet red from battle,
And after the shouting bitter reflection.

Before Geraint, the foe's oppressor,
I saw horses with trappings of white,
And after the shouting a bitter shroud.

At Llongborth I saw vultures
And corpses, too many, carried away,
And men all red where Geraint charged.

At Llongborth I saw slaughter,
Frightened men and bloody heads
Before Geraint, his father's great son.

At Llongborth I saw spurs,
And men not afraid of spears,
And wine drunk from sparkling glass.

At Llongborth I saw armour,
Men, and blood being spilt,
And after the shouting a bitter burial.

At Llongborth I saw Arthur.
Brave men who struck with steel.
An emperor commanding the battle.

At Llongborth Geraint fell,
And brave men from lowland Devon.
Before they were killed, they killed.

Fast were the horses that Geraint rode,
Long-legged, and fed upon wheat.
They were red, and they moved like milk-white eagles.

Fast were the horses that Geraint rode,
Long-legged, and fed upon grain.
They were red, and they moved like jet-black eagles.

Fast were the horses that Geraint rode,
Long-legged, and nourished on grain.
They were red, and they moved like crimson eagles.

Fast were the horses that Geraint rode,
Long-legged, devourers of grain.
They were red, and they moved like white eagles.

Fast were the horses that Geraint rode,
Long-legged, swift as the stag.
The roar of a fire on a barren mountain.

Fast were the horses that Geraint rode,
Long-legged, greedy for grain,
Gray, their hair tipped with silver.

Fast were the horses that Geraint rode,
Long-legged, worthy of grain.
They were red, and they moved like gray eagles.

Fast were the horses that Geraint rode,
Long-legged, fed upon grain.
They were red, and they moved like brown eagles.

When Geraint was born, heaven's gates were open.
Christ gave what was asked:
A noble face, the glory of Britain.

(Translated by Professor Carl Lofmark in *Bards and Heroes*, Llanerch)

The Anglo-Saxon Chronicle has the following entry for the year 501:

> In this year Port and his two sons, Bieda and Maegla, came with two ships
> to Britain at the place which is called Portesmutha, and slew a young
> Briton, a very noble man.

Dr John Morris in *The Age of Arthur* is convinced that poem and
chronicle refer to the same battle and that Llongborth is Portchester/
Portsmouth Harbour:

> Llongborth is the 'ship port'. Llong in Welsh carries the general meaning of
> ships of all sorts; but when the word was first taken into British from Latin
> it had the more precise meaning of warship, longa navis. A port of warships,
> a naval base where a prince from Devon fought and died in the fifth cen-
> tury, can hardly be other than Portchester, the westernmost of the Saxon
> Shore forts listed in the Notitia, at the head of Portsmouth Harbour.

John Morris points out that Geraint is listed in the genealogies as a
Prince of Dumnonia, later called Dyfneint in Welsh and Devon in English
and that one of Port's sons (Maegla) has a British name. He gives an impressive array of circumstantial evidence to support a theory that some form of
British-Saxon alliance held the strategically important Portchester and that
the battle was an unsuccessful attack on this base by Dumnonian forces. The
Anglo-British alliance seems to have resulted in the founding of the House
of Wessex by a ruler with a British name – Cerdic – an interesting situation
stimulatingly developed by several modern 'Arthurian' novelists.

The poem seems to refer to an association between Geraint and Arthur
in a cavalry-led attack on Llongborth by Christian troops from Devon.
As we have seen, the Welsh legendary Arthurian material and Geoffrey of
Monmouth frequently refer to Arthur's close connection with the rulers
of Dumnonia.

The Book of Taliesin contains poems which refer to Uther Pendragon,
to Arthur's horse, to a bard who blesses Arthur and to a quest by Arthur
into the Otherworld in search of a magic cauldron, which may be a prototype of the Holy Grail story.

As well as the poem *Y Gododdin*, already referred to, *The Book of Aneirin* has an allusion to the porc Trwyth, a central feature of the prose tale
'How Culhwch Won Olwen' in *The Mabinogion*.

The Black Book of Carmarthen has the first hint of Arthur's immortality in a poem entitled 'The Song of the Graves':

> Osvran's son's grave at Camlan,
> After many a slaughter,
> Bedwyr's grave in Allt Tryvan.
> A grave for March, a grave for Gwythur,
> A grave for Gwgawn of the ruddy sword,
> Concealed until doomsday, the grave of Arthur.

The Black Book also contains a fragment of a dialogue between Arthur and the porter of his hillfort. Arthur's companions are Kei and Bedwyr. There is also a poem referring to the death of Arthur's son:

> I was there where Llacheu fell,
> Arthur's son famed in song,
> When ravens flocked on the gore.

The Red Book of Hergest features a number of triads, which were probably memory-aids for bards, including 'The Three Evil Discoveries of Britain':

> One was that of Arthur, who took away the head of Bran the Blessed from the White Hill; he did not like the island to be guarded by another might than his own:

This refers to the tradition mentioned in *The Mabinogion* that Bran instructed his head to be buried in the White Hill (where the Tower of London is now) to protect the Island of the Mighty from invasion. The name Bran means raven and there must be a connection between this legend and the subsequent tradition that Britain's safety depended on the ravens staying at the Tower. Sir Winston Churchill gave instructions for the especial care of the ravens in the Tower during the Second World War and we must be dealing here with one our most ancient pieces of folklore.

A number of triads deal with traditions of the abduction of Guinevere and the causes of the Battle of Camlann, such as the Three Furious Blows of Britain, ('The slap which Gwenhwyvach gave Gwenhwyvar, and which caused the Battle of Camlann') and The Three Costly Pillages:

The first was when Medrawd went to Galliwig; he did not leave enough meat and drink in the court to sustain a fly, but consumed and wasted it all; and he dragged Gwenhwyvar from her throne, and committed adultery with her. The second was when Arthur went to the court of Medrawd; he left neither meat nor drink that he did not destroy; and he killed every living thing in the hundred, both man and beast.

Galliwig refers to Castle Killibury, a Cornish hillfort, now partly destroyed and a farm site.

The Black Book of Carmarthen includes a number of poems featuring the persona of the bard Myrddin. The Welsh Annals has an entry for the year 573:

The battle of Arfderydd between the sons of Eliffer and Gwenddolau son of Ceidio; in which battle Gwenddolau fell; Merlinus went mad.

This Battle of Arthuret, a Cumbrian village on the Scottish border, is referred to in the Welsh triads as one of the 'Three Futile Battles' because it was fought over 'a Lark's Nest'. This is a sophisticated and grim play on words typical of Welsh poetry, as the battle was fought because of a dispute over the ownership of the Fort of Caerlaverock, south of Dumfries on the Solway Firth, the name of which means 'The Fort of the Lark'. From the poetic references, Gwenddolau appears to have been both Merlin's tribal chief and kinsman. Merlin somehow betrayed him before or during the battle and suffered exile in the Caledonian Forest during which he is supposed to have written inspired poetry. The story does merge into archetypal European myth and legend (another example is the Irish legend of Lailoken) and the Merlin or Myrddin of the poems in *The Black Book* appears to be being used as a persona, much as T.S. Eliot uses the Prufrock character. On the mythical level a certain amount of druidic and bardic lore seems to have survived in the Merlin figure and Geoffrey of Monmouth develops the Merlin figure in an interesting way in the twelfth century.

THE MABINOGION

The Red Book of Hergest also contains a collection of prose tales in Welsh (also found in *The White Book of Rhydderch*) known since Lady Charlotte Guest's translation of them in the 1840s as *The Mabinogion*. Five of these stories concern Arthur. *The White Book* is thought to be thirteenth-century and *The Red Book* fourteenth-century, but scholars consider them to be transcripts of twelfth-century written texts which contain still older material from earlier written or oral sources. Four of the stories show the influence of French romance (three of them have parallel versions in Chretien De Troyes' Arthurian romances of the twelfth century). The remaining tale, 'How Culhwch Won Olwen', is pre-romance, with pagan and folklore elements and clear evidence of oral tradition. It has strong claims to be the earliest complete surviving story which prominently features Arthur.

The folk tale elements in 'How Culhwch Won Olwen' include: the jealous stepmother, the curse or 'swearing of a destiny', the asking of a boon (which survives into the romance genre), the achieving of difficult or seemingly impossible tasks, talking animals who help mankind, the hunting of a supernatural beast and the seeking of a giant's daughter to marry.

Pagan elements include the swearing of an oath on natural phenomena (rather than by God, the Virgin or the saints):

> ... you shall have the boon which head and tongue request, so far as the wind dries, so far as the rain moistens, so far as the sun rises, so far as the sea swells, so far as the earth reaches, apart from my ship, my mantle, my sword Caledfwlch, my spear Rhongomyniad, my shield Wynebgwrthucher, my knife Carnwennan and my wife Gwenhwyvar ...

Arthur makes this offer as response to an unspecified request for help from his cousin Culhwch, who has with difficulty obtained entrance to Arthur's hillfort during the New Year ceremonies. Culhwch has been cursed by his step-mother into falling in love with a giant's daughter whom he has never seen and whose marriage would cause the giant's death – clear folklore motifs. Arthur's porter, Glewlwyd, whom we also meet in Welsh poetry, tries to prevent Culhwch from bursting in on the feast:

> Knife has gone into meat, and drink into horn, and there is a gathering in the Hall of Arthur. Nobody can enter apart from a lawful king or a craftsman providing his skills. You shall have mash for your dogs and corn for your horse, and hot peppered chops and plenty of wine and delightful songs; you will be served with food sufficient for fifty men in the hospice

with the strangers and men from foreign lands who bring no craft, and you
shall have a woman to sleep with and entertaining songs to listen to.

This reflects early heroic society with its graded hospitality for all-
comers and its emphasis on the important status of the craftsman. The
ready availability of women and 'hot peppered chops' are less likely to
be so blatantly referred to in the more sophisticated French romances.
Culhwch's boon is requested in front of two hundred of Arthur's followers, who are listed and were presumably originally recited as a memory
feat for a bard in an oral tale. Given prominent place are Cei and Bedwyr
(the Kay and Bedivere of Geoffrey of Monmouth and later stories) and
Gwalchmei, the prototype of Gawain who is said to never come home
without his quest.

The poetic description of Olwen emphasises her beauty in similes
from the natural world and has a freshness which contrasts with some of
the more ornate, bejewelled and artificial descriptions of beautiful ladies
in the later Arthurian romances:

> More yellow was her hair than the flower of the broom. More white was
> her flesh than the foam of the wave. More white were her palms and fin-
> gers than the marsh trefoil rising through the delicate gravel of a gushing
> spring. Her eyes were peerlessly beautiful, surpassing those of the mewed
> hawk and the triple-mewed falcon. More white were her breasts than the
> breast of the white swan. More red were her cheeks than the reddest fox-
> gloves. Whoever saw her was bound to fall in love with her.

In true folktale style the giant makes the fulfilment of many impossible tasks the condition of marrying his daughter to Culhwch, who
again invokes the help of Arthur and his followers. Arthur himself takes
a prominent part in the hunting of the pig Twrch Trwyth (a transformed
prince) and in obtaining of the blood of the Black Witch (who in more
recent times has been identified with Wookey Hole) which he does by
throwing his dagger Carnwenan at her and slicing her in half.

'The Lady of the Fountain' has the historical Owain of Rheged as
its hero. He and his equally famous father Urien won undying fame in
fighting against the Saxons in the North in the post-Arthurian period in
the mid and late sixth century. There are a number of surviving poems
about these warrior-chieftains, some attributed to the bard Taliesin. Both

these heroes are posthumously co-opted into the Knights of the Round Table and by one of the strangest twists in Arthurian legends Urien and Owain are given Morgan Le Fay as respectively wife and mother. Morgan is a purely mythological and religious Celtic figure, who can be traced back through Breton and Welsh mythology to the Irish war goddess, the Morrigan, who in the form of a raven perched on the body of the hero Cuchulain to indicate his death (as shown in the famous statue in the Dublin Post Office).

'The Lady of the Fountain' has many ancient pre-Arthurian elements, including traces of moon worship and a matrilinear society, though this could also reflect the descent through the female line adopted by necessity at times in the new Crusader states in the Holy Land. The extraordinary magic fountain in the story is the Fontaine de Barenton in the Foret de Paimpont in Brittany, which is thought to have been a druidic sacred place, and has much folklore pertaining to it and to the adjacent stone slab which can be 'activated', according to tradition, by having water poured onto it. Owain's state of forgetfulness between his married home in Brittany and Arthur's Court at Caerleon is redolent of Celtic stories of heroes straying into the otherworld and sometimes finding a mate there. Chretien De Troyes used the same material for his twelfth-century romance *Ivain*. Although the inspiration for the story is Celtic legend and religious belief, the French romance has undoubtedly influenced the Welsh form as we have it today. The character of Kay (the typical boasting champion of oral literature in the Welsh poems and in 'Culhwch and Olwen') is already shown as the unpleasant and ineffectual braggart he becomes in the sophisticated French Arthurian romances. So there has been cross-fertilisation and/or a common source, possibly Breton.

Two other stories in *The Mabinogion*, 'Geraint and Enid' and 'Peredur', find their counterparts in romances by Chretien called 'Eric and Enide' and 'Perceval' and again we have chicken and egg situations as to which came first in their surviving forms. The final Arthurian story in *The Mabinogion* is 'The Dream of Rhonaby', which would seem to be a newly written story, using the fashionable late medieval dream-vision structure, but which has some earlier legendary material in it, such as Owain's magic flock of ravens (presumably inherited from his supernatural mother).

Although well known in Wales, *The Mabinogion* had to await translation by Lady Charlotte Guest in the 1840s before influencing versions of the Arthurian story in English starting with Tennyson.

5 Geoffrey of Monmouth

In 1136 a magister (MA) and lecturer at St George's College, Oxford (a forerunner of the University of Oxford), seeking preferment to a high ecclesiastical post, produced a racily-written popular history of Britain which would be acceptable to his Norman masters. He provided an heroic past for their new country to rival the Charlemagne epics of the French and cast the conquered Anglo-Saxons in the role of 'baddies'.

Geoffrey of Monmouth's *History of the Kings of Britain* had enormous influence – over two hundred manuscript copies of it still survive – and a considerable portion of his book deals with 'King' Arthur. Geoffrey wrote in Latin, but twenty years later a cleric from Jersey, Wace, expanded Geoffrey's work into about 15,000 French octosyllabic lines under the title of *Le Roman de Brut*, and dedicated it to Eleanor of Aquitaine. Wace's additions comment on a strong Breton oral tradition concerning Arthur including the idea of an Arthurian second coming. Wace also supplies the first reference to the Round Table ('of which the Britons tell many fabulous tales'), also drawn from folk tradition. Geoffrey of Monmouth and Wace had a strong influence on the writers of French Arthurian romances.

Wace's work was in turn translated into English alliterative poetry at the end of the twelfth century by Layamon, a priest at Arley Regis in Worcestershire. And so for the first time Arthur became a national hero for the English, against whom Arthur had spent his career fighting. Layamon cuts out much of the emerging chivalric and romantic elements in Wace and introduces brutal scenes and comments, such as Arthur punishing a knight by having the noses of women related to him cut off and Gawain's wish to have Guinevere torn apart by wild horses. We are already seeing how the Arthurian stories are adapted by different writers to reflect their own cultures and preoccupations and Layamon's story is more reflective of an heroic, violent and vengeful society than Wace's, despite being written forty years later.

Geoffrey of Monmouth's signature, surviving in several Oxford charters, was 'Geoffrey Arthur', which is interpreted as signifying that his father was called Arthur; thus Geoffrey is likely to be at least of part

Welsh or Breton stock. Although in the seventh century 'Arthur' had become a popular name amongst the Welsh ruling classes (further circumstantial evidence of our Arthur's existence and status), by the eleventh and twelfth centuries the name 'Arthur' was more popular in Brittany than in Wales. At the end of the twelfth century, Constance of Brittany named her son Arthur (assassinated at the instigation of King John according to Shakespeare's chronicle sources) in a political gesture aimed at popular support.

A significant proportion of Duke William's forces at Hastings were Breton and these partly justified the invasion by claiming they were returning to the homeland from which they had been ousted by the Saxons. After the Conquest there was some intermarriage between Normans and Bretons and the Welsh. Even after political difficulties between Norman and Welsh began to emerge, the cultural interchange of ideas remained and the Normans had a greater respect for Welsh culture than for that of the Anglo–Saxons, which they did their best to eliminate.

Therefore it was understandable that the Normans should turn to British heroes such as Arthur (whom they had already heard about from their Breton allies) to establish a cultural pedigree for their new kingdom to rival that of France. Breton and Welsh poets and storytellers became welcome in Normandy and France and at the English court. One such real-life minstrel, Bleheris, enters Arthurian romance as Merlin's mage and instructor, Master Bleys.

Some of Geoffrey's forebears therefore possibly came over with Duke William or in the wake of the Norman Conquest and we know that many Bretons moved into Wales in these years. But we should not overlook the distinct possibility that Geoffrey was at least part Welsh and he was presumably born at Monmouth. He certainly had an intimate knowledge of Caerleon which is featured in his book as Arthur's capital and extensively described in its contemporary twelfth-century context. The Roman remains, including the amphitheatre known locally as 'King Arthur's Round Table' since 1405, were for many years interpreted as being Arthurian. Geoffrey eventually got his preferment and was known to be in London receiving his appointment as Bishop of the Welsh see of St Asaph in 1051. The Normans did not usually appoint Welshmen as bishops of Welsh sees, which is another point in favour of Geoffrey being of Breton or mixed Breton–Norman stock. The strong Breton bias in his book and the possible use of lost Breton sources or folklore are further factors in favour of this.

Many historians have been reluctant to take Geoffrey seriously, even as a transmitter of traditions. This is a pity as he is a vital link in the chain of Arthurian cultural development and he does incorporate identifiable chronicle traditions as well as much interesting material not found previously elsewhere which may have traditional and even historical significance. Because so much of the content of *The History of the Kings of Britain* is fabulous or exaggerated, many historians have ignored it. Literary scholars, however, have always been sceptical about the claim of historians that Geoffrey invented everything – that just wasn't the way with medieval writers. That much of what Geoffrey tells us is historically suspect doesn't mean that Geoffrey invented it all. For those interested in the development of the Arthurian legends and their interaction with culture, where Geoffrey got his material from is of supreme importance. And the answer once again seems to be – from the Celts. Geoffrey actually tells us that he had a written source:

> Walter, Archdeacon of Oxford, a man skilled in the art of oratory and knowledgeable about the history of foreign countries, gave me a particular ancient book written in the language of the Britons. This book, attractively written to give a consecutive and clear narrative, outlined all the deeds of these men, from Brutus, the first King of the Britons, down to Cadwalo. At the request of Walter, I have ... translated the book into Latin, although certainly I have used my own expressions and my own homely style and I have gathered no gaudy flowers of speech in other men's gardens.

Walter was Provost of St George's College in Oxford and Geoffrey's boss and his name appears as co-signatory of five charters with Geoffrey. It seems inconceivable that Geoffrey should publicly claim to have received source material from his boss (who would doubtless have read the book and probably discussed its writing) unless this had happened. Geoffrey says that Walter brought the book *'ex Britannia'*. The 'language of the Britons' could mean Welsh, Breton or Cornish and Peter Berresford Ellis in his recent book *Celt and Saxon* thinks he has tracked down the book – a Cornish history listed in the Vatican library. This is an interesting piece of research, particularly in view of the amount of Cornish material in the Arthurian sections of Geoffrey of Monmouth's book. The objection that Geoffrey's book contains some material which could not have been in an ancient source does not stand up because one would expect a medieval author (and particularly Geoffrey) to elaborate and add to what might have been a small source book. And the source book need not have been as ancient as Geoffrey thought.

We can also show that Geoffrey is using material from Virgil, Gildas, Prosper, Bede and Nennius. Geoffrey's account of the Arthurian battles seems to be an embroidery of the list in Nennius, though an independent lost source is a possibility. An enormous amount of early chronicles and literature has been lost and William of Malmesbury, a reputable and respected historian, researched in the library at Glastonbury Abbey a few years before Geoffrey's book and, although initially a sceptic, became convinced by what he found there that Arthur was an historical figure.

Geoffrey certainly did extensively embroider and elaborate his sources and his affinity for Celtic folk tale and the supernatural (such as the Giant of Mont Saint Michel episode) did discredit him with some of his more serious contemporaries. Gerald of Wales, for example, tells how a patient was cured from diabolical fits by having a Bible placed on his chest. When this was replaced by a copy of Geoffrey's book, the fits continued! So historians are justified in being wary of Geoffrey, but not in ignoring him.

Geoffrey seems to have had a lifelong interest in Merlin. His earliest known works were a series of 'Prophecies of Merlin' which he later incorporated into the *History*. He also replaces Ambrosius by Merlin in a tale told by Nennius. In Geoffrey's *History* it is the young Merlin who is brought before Vortigern to be sacrificed to consecrate the building of Vortigern's castle at Dinas Emrys (a site named after Ambrosius whose Welsh folklore name is Emrys). Merlin's impressive diagnosis that the castle is collapsing because it stands over a pool of water in which two dragons, symbolising the Celts and Saxons, are fighting, secures him a job as a sort of latter-day druidic adviser to Vortigern and his successors – Ambrosius, Uther and Arthur.

Geoffrey's version of the conception of Merlin through the liaison of a demon incubus and a nun has affinities with the *Merlin* of the Burgundian poet Robert De Boron writing at the end of the century. It is perhaps a Christian attempt to explain powers which traditionally go back to Celtic religion and druidism.

As in the chronicle sources, the fightback against Hengist and the Saxons is led by Ambrosius, but Geoffrey adds in Uther as Ambrosius's brother and successor and father to Arthur; the brothers return from exile in Brittany. Few scholars have tried to prove the existence of Uther, but he is mentioned in one early Welsh poem. And there is a Cumbrian tradition that Pendragon Castle in Cumbria stands on the site of an earlier fort built by Uther, whose attempts to change the course of the River Eden to form a moat are said to have given rise to a local rhyme:

> Let Uther Pendragon do what he can,
> Eden will run where Eden ran

The present ruins are the remains of a castle built by Hugh de Morville, one of the murderers of Becket and the castle is referred to in Malory's *Le Morte D'Arthur* as being given as a gift by Lancelot to a deserving knight. The name 'Cumbria' is Celtic ('land of the Cymri') and the population remained largely Celtic until the Norse influx and many Celtic traditions survive.

Merlin's magical work includes the re-siting of Stonehenge, known as 'The Giants' Dance', from Ireland to Stonehenge to commemorate the slaying of the 300 noblemen by Hengist, but his most famous achievement is to arrange the conception of Arthur.

In Geoffrey's *History*, Uther's right-hand man is the Duke of Cornwall, a connection which carries on into the reign of Arthur, whose right-hand man is Duke Cador of Cornwall, an historical king of Dumnonia and father to Arthur's 'successor', Constantine, who was known to Gildas. Geoffrey, through his Breton or Cornish sources, may well be reflecting some genuine historical alliance between Arthur and his predecessors and Dumnonia.

In Geoffrey's account the support between Uther and Gorlois breaks down because Uther takes a fancy to Gorlois's wife, Ygerna, at a feast in London. Gorlois flees back to his Cornish Kingdom with his wife to take refuge until he can receive help from Ireland, pursued by Uther and his army:

> He left her in the castle of Tintagel, on the sea-coast, which he thought to be the most secure place in his kingdom. He himself took refuge in a fort named Dimilioc, so that, if disaster befell, they should not both be endangered together. When the King learnt of this, he besieged Gorlois' encampment and guarded every way of approach.

Ulfin tells Uther that Tintagel is impregnable:

> No earthly power can enable us to get at her inside the fortress of Tintagel.
> The castle is built high above the sea, which surrounds it on all sides. The
> only other way in is by a narrow rocky path, which three armed soldiers
> could defend against you, even if you had the whole kingdom of Britain
> at your side.

Uther has to resort to unearthly power, that of Merlin's magic, to transform him into the likeness of Gorlois in order to sleep with Ygerna so that she can conceive the future King Arthur. We are here in the realm of Celtic shape-shifting and European myth where a god takes on human form in order to sire a hero. On a purely practical level, Geoffrey's story breaks down because the death of Gorlois the same night as the conception would seem to render the whole ploy unnecessary, since Uther then weds Ygerna. This flaw suggests that Geoffrey did not invent the whole thing, but is rather trying to weld together disparate material – myth with historical legend.

Another interesting possibility is that the whole story suggests a doubt about Arthur's kingly or even aristocratic birth and the need to provide a superior pedigree for him, which would fit in with the Welsh Saints' Lives calling him a *tyrannus*. Such a requirement might date back to Arthur's day, but could also reflect the needs of storytellers at any stage in the development of the legend, trying to inflate the pedigree of their hero by imbuing him with supernatural birth, royal blood and legitimacy.

The whole scenario also raises questions of illegitimacy which are dramatically exploited by the later French writers and by Malory. If Arthur is conceived when Gorlois is still alive, then he is a bastard and cannot inherit the kingdom according to later medieval French and English practice. But if Gorlois is dead when Arthur is conceived then he can be legitimised by the marriage of his parents before his birth. The importance of the timing of the conception is made graphically explicit in the film *Excalibur*. Geoffrey's lack of concern for this may reflect a more easy-going approach in his day to illegitimacy (William the Conqueror was a bastard who inherited Normandy).

The mythical elements in Arthur's conception have led most historians to assume that Arthur's connection with Tintagel is pure invention on Geoffrey's part. The usual view has been that Geoffrey took his summer holidays on the north Cornish coast, saw the beginnings of a Norman Castle there and decided this would make a good setting for the birth of Arthur. Many writers on the site discounted the possibility of Celtic or earlier fortifications or of any historical importance for the site in Romano-Celtic times.

Several Cornish local scholars did persist in advocating a Roman connection – perhaps a trading post or fort – due to the discovery of two Roman milestones close to the Trevena–Boscastle road. Professor Raleigh Radford excavated the Tintagel site in the 1930s and suggested that some overgrown buildings outside of the Castle might be a Celtic monastery. The past twenty years have seen exciting discoveries at Tintagel and an expert assessment of these is found in Professor Charles Thomas's *Tintagel: Arthur and Archaeology*.

Professor Thomas's view of the current evidence is that Tintagel Castle was built for Richard Earl of Cornwall about 1230, not for any strategic purpose but because of Richard's interest in Arthurian legends (Richard was something of a scholar). The thirteenth-century remains do at points seem to be built onto something earlier, so we may not have heard the last of this. But, according to Professor Thomas, there was no Norman castle to inspire Geoffrey if he came to Tintagel. However Professor Thomas also shows that there are the remains of a ditch going back to the post-Roman period, the implication being that we are dealing with a Celtic fortified site.

Although the idea of a monastery is now discredited, some of the stone buildings (including a chapel on the headland) pre-date Geoffrey and the 1983 fire on the headland revealed evidence of many timber buildings on slate foundations which may be as early as the fifth century, but need to be thoroughly excavated. Fifth- or sixth-century Christian mound burials in the church also point to the likelihood that the site may have been the stronghold of a Dumnonian Christian Celtic chieftain and literature and legend ascribes it to King Mark as well as to Gorlois. The enormous finds of pottery do also suggest an even earlier Roman connection of some kind, such as a trading station.

Professor Thomas's book is of enormous help in solving problems, disbanding misconceptions and clarifying the issues which are still to be resolved concerning the Tintagel site. He shows that Tintagel was probably the most important site in Cornwall in the Arthurian period and that it was very likely a Roman trading station linked to, or developing into a chieftain's stronghold. Professor Thomas, however, remains convinced that there is no Arthurian connection.

But does not the new evidence, including Professor Thomas's own work and analysis, allow for a 'discourse' (to use his own term in his book) for an Arthurian connection at least in legend and that perhaps Geoffrey of Monmouth read about such a connection rather than inventing it? Geoffrey's account does sound like an eye-witness description, but Geoffrey could have taken the defensive description from someone else or he may have visited Tintagel because his curiosity was aroused. It is likely that Geoffrey knew what modern historians have only just become aware of, that Tintagel was a site of major importance.

Moreover there is a strong Arthurian connection with Dumnonia in the Welsh sources as well as in the Cornish or Breton material with which Geoffrey is dealing.

Another element of Arthur's story which first clearly emerges in Geoffrey's work, is his extraordinary defeat of the Emperor Lucius of Rome. It is tempting to think that Geoffrey is dealing with Breton material here, which focuses on the European mainland and there may be a confusion with earlier leaders of Roman Britain such as Maximus who led troops from Britain against the Roman Emperor of the West and killed and succeeded him. There are, however, some references to Arthur's continental campaign in Welsh poems which are difficult to date. The manuscripts are later than Geoffrey, but the poems themselves could pre-date Geoffrey and represent an independent Welsh tradition of this curious campaign.

Geoffrey places Arthur's Gallic wars during the reign of the Emperor of the East, Leo (457-474), which conflicts with all the other likely dating we have for Arthur's career and with Geoffrey's own date for Arthur's death of 542:

> Arthur himself, our celebrated King, was mortally wounded and taken off
> to the Isle of Avalon, so that his wounds might be attended to. He passed
> the crown of Britain to his cousin Constantine, the son of Cador Duke of
> Cornwall: this was in the year 542 after our Lord's Incarnation.

The historical Constantine was ruling a small kingdom in the west at about this date. This is also the first reference to Avalon, the Isle of Apples, a form of the Celtic Otherworld. In Geoffrey's later work, *Vita Merlini*, there is a substantial account of the island, ruled over by Morgan Le Fay, described by the bard Taliesin:

The island of Apples is called by men the Fortunate Isle because it produces everything needful. The fields there have no need of farmers to plough them and nature provides all cultivation unassisted. Grain and grapes are produced without nurture and apple trees grow in the woods ... The earth of its own accord brings forth ... all things in superabundance ... There, after the battle of Camlann, we took the wounded Arthur ... and Morgan received us with appropriate honour. She placed the king on a golden bed in her own chamber and with her own noble hand uncovered the wound, and gazed at it for a long while. At last she said that he could be restored to health if he stayed with her for a long time and was subject to her healing art. With rejoicing, therefore, we committed the king to her keeping, and returned, giving our sails to the favouring winds.

This also gives the origin of the 'once and future king' legend, which is also obliquely referred to in Welsh poetry. An interesting near-contemporary reference to Breton and Cornish beliefs that Arthur would come again is given by Hermann De Tournai in his 1146 account of a visit to Britain by Canons of Laon in 1113, bringing a miracle-working shrine of Our Lady of Laon to raise funds. In Devon they were told they were in King Arthur's land and shown 'Arthur's Chair' and 'Arthur's Oven'. At Bodmin a dispute arose with a man with a withered arm: 'Just as the Bretons are wont to wrangle with the French on behalf of King Arthur', so the man maintained that Arthur still lived. A fight developed, Our Lady was offended and the man was not healed.

'Merlin taketh the child Arthur into his keeping.' *Drawing by Aubrey Beardsley*

6 Glastonbury and Avalon

At the end of the last chapter we saw how the concept of Arthur as a 'once and future king' developed among the Celtic peoples. The dying yet reviving figure in the Celtic Otherworld is a relic of Celtic paganism which pre-dates the Christian Arthur and yet which has common ground with the Christian concept of the second coming. And Arthur is an overtly Christian ruler in nearly all literary treatments from the Middle Ages through to Tennyson's Christ-like Arthur in *Idylls of the King* – as indeed he almost certainly was historically. The concept of the second coming is so rooted in world mythology that one suspects it is a profound archetypal need of humankind. It is this mythological dimension which gives Arthur the legendary edge over other equally heroic figures such as Alfred the Great.

The Celts may not have originally conceived Avalon as a place which could be physically identified. Dr Miranda Green suggests that it may derive from Irish mythology, in which the sea-god Manannan ruled an Otherworld island called Emhain Ablach ('Emhain of the Apple Trees'). An 'Ynis (Isle) Avallach' is mentioned in Welsh poetry and there is a Cumbrian tradition of an Otherworld lake-ruler Avallach.

In 1191, in what appears to have been one of the great medieval forgeries at which the Abbey of Glastonbury was so adept, the Abbot announced to a startled world the finding of the bodies of Arthur and Guinevere in the old monks' cemetery together with a small lead cross which identified the site as The Isle of Avalon. Two excellent descriptions and debates of the evidence are found in Leslie Alcock's *Arthur's Britain* and Philip Rahtz's *Glastonbury*.

Money seems to have been the root cause of events. In 1184 a fire destroyed the 'Old Church' of St Mary's and most of the other buildings, including the library and many of the books. The leaders of the Abbey appealed to King Henry II for help in funds for rebuilding. Henry responded by allowing the Abbey revenues to be used; he also apparently advised the monks to find the body of King Arthur which would be a useful fund-raising tourist attraction. Henry said that 'an ancient Welsh bard' had revealed to him the position of the tomb. If this is correct then it indicates an earlier Celtic tradition of Arthur's burial at Glastonbury which inspired the forgery.

By a delightful paradox, Gerald of Wales, who was so critical of the excesses of Geoffrey of Monmouth's imagination, gives the earliest account and swallows a forgery much more serious than anything perpetrated by Geoffrey's pen, hook, line and sinker. This is a translation of Gerald's Latin account, written within a few months of the excavation:

> King Arthur's body was discovered in our own times at Glastonbury, entombed deep in the earth in a hollow oak between two stone pyramids ... Within was a cross of lead ... fixed on the under side of the stone ... I have touched the letters engraved upon it, which do not stand out, but are turned inwards towards the stone. They run as follows: 'Here lies buried the famous King Arthur, with Guinevere his second wife, in the Isle of Avalon'.
>
> ...Two thirds of the tomb contained the bones of the man, while the remaining third towards the foot contained the bones of the woman placed apart. They discovered a yellow tress of woman's hair still retaining its colour and freshness; but when a certain monk snatched at it greedily, it immediately crumbled into dust ... Arthur's bones were so large that his shank-bone, when placed against that of the tallest man present, reached a good three inches above his knee ... There were ten wounds or more, all of which were healed, apart from one larger than the others, which had made a huge gash.

Another contemporary chronicler, Ralph of Coggeshall, says the burial was *'in quodam vetustissimo sarcophago'* ('in an ancient sarcophagus') and he omits any reference to Guinevere's presence in the tomb or on the cross. His version of the inscription is:

> *Hic iacet inclitus rex Arturius*
> *in insula Avallonis sepultus.*
> ('Here lies the famous king Arthur, buried in the isle of Avalon.')

Later transcriptions and drawings of the cross make no reference to Guinevere and it is tempting to follow Ralph's version rather than Gerald's, though Professor Rahtz and Dr Antonia Gransden have both recently suggested that Gerald was an eye-witness (though without any evidence). The idea of Arthur and Guinevere being buried together is unusual, perhaps unique, in Arthurian folklore and literature. However, support for Gerald comes in an account in 1278 of a visit by Edward I and Queen Eleanor to Glastonbury to witness the opening of the tomb:

> And there separately in two chests painted with their images and arms, were found the bones of Arthur of wonderful size and the bones of Queen Guinevere of wonderful beauty.

The account mentions that the next day the King and Queen wrapped the bones in precious stuff and returned them to the their chests in a black marble mausoleum in front of the altar. Curiously their 'heads and cheeks' were kept out 'on account of the devotion of the people'. Shades of the Celtic cult of the head! Indeed the whole concept of the veneration of the relics of Arthur and Guinevere is unusual as they were not saints and shows their extraordinary prestige in legend. The prosperity of the Abbey flourished, aided by other forged and faked celebrity connections.

The site where the monks dug to 'recover' the body can be identified with certainty. Professor Alcock summarises the evidence as follows:

> The careful description of the twelfth-century historian William of Malmesbury makes it clear that the two 'pyramids' which flanked the burial were in fact standing crosses, respectively four and five stages high. They stood in the ancient cemetery south of the Lady Chapel. Trenching there in 1962 disclosed firstly a pit apparently about five feet across, from which a great cross might have been removed; then, about ten feet further south, traces of an early mausoleum, which had already been demolished in the tenth century; and third, between the mausoleum and the pit, a large irregular hole which had been dug out and then shortly afterwards refilled in the 1180s or 1190s. The evidence for this precise date is the occurrence in the hole of masons' chippings of the Doulton stone which was used only in building the Lady Chapel in 1184-9. The masons' chippings can scarcely have lain around the area for any length of time. All this points to the irregular hole being the one from which the bones claimed as those of Arthur and Guinevere were exhumed in 1191.
> (*Arthur's Britain* Penguin)

The existence of the cross can also be verified; it was last heard of in Glastonbury in the late seventeenth century according to Professor

Rahtz and in Wells in the eighteenth century according to Professor Alcock and Geoffrey Ashe, who has traced it to the possession of Mr Hugh-
es, one of the Cathedral clergy. The antiquarian John Leland saw it about
1542 and gives the same transcription as Gerald, with the omission of the
reference to Guinevere. Camden includes it in his first five editions of
his *Britannia* (1586-1600) and in his sixth edition publishes a drawing of
it. Professor Alcock considers that the lettering is of tenth-century style
and that it is either a forgery (tenth-century lettering being probably the
earliest available at Glastonbury after the fire) or a product of Dunstan's
day. His ingenious theory is that Abbot Dunstan, in his alterations to the
Abbey graveyard, came across Arthur's grave with a simple inscription
marker with a Latin format of something like 'Here buried lies Arthur',
appropriate to the early sixth century and that Dunstan was responsible
for the slightly more elaborate wording of a replacement cross which was
found by the excavators.

Professor Rahtz suspects that the style of the lettering may even be
contemporary and is convinced that the cross is a forgery: 'any attempts
to validate it are wishful thinking by those who believe in the existence
of Arthur and his connection with Glastonbury'.

The Arthurian Encyclopedia points out that 'the standard twelfth-century Latinisation of "Arthur" was not *Arturius*, as on the cross, but *Arturus*
as in Geoffrey' (of Monmouth). Up to 1191, "Arturius" can only be paralleled in Adamnan's seventh-century *Life of St Columba*, where the person
referred to is Prince Arthur of Argyll. In other words, it occurs only as a
very early form.'

Professor Rahtz is probably correct about the forgery, but surely
Professor Alcock is right to emphasise that Arthur is connected with
Glastonbury before the 'discovery' of his grave. Not only is there the
comment by Henry II, but, as we have seen in the section on Saints'
Lives, Caradoc of Llancarfan locates the abduction of Guinevere to Glastonbury. Other early tales (though difficult to date) connect Arthur with
Beckery Chapel in Glastonbury and with the apparent death of Ider
(a knight who helps to rescue Guinevere on the Modena Archivolt in
another of the abduction stories) at nearby Brent Knoll; Arthur paid for
twenty-four monks from Glastonbury to pray for Ider's soul and donated
Brent Knoll to the Abbey. Arthur's legendary connection with Glastonbury does not cease if his exhumation is proved a forgery – indeed the
exhumation was probably caused by the legend.

It would be intriguing to know whether Glastonbury was regarded as an Otherworld site or indeed as Avalon before the 'discovery' of Arthur's tomb. The location would have been nearly surrounded by water at times in Arthur's day and 400 years earlier there were advanced civilisations in the Glastonbury Lake Villages which might have left legends behind them. The legend of St Collum meeting Gwnn Ap Nudd, son of the God Nodens (who had a temple across the Severn at Lydney), the dedication of the Tor top church to St Michael, the Archangel Militant, and the Chalice Well all suggest a Celtic religious site. In Chretien De Troyes's *Lancelot* (1170) Guinevere is abducted to the Otherworld (like Persephone). Perhaps Caradoc, in locating her abduction at Glastonbury, was drawing on a known tradition as Glastonbury as an Otherworld citadel. Celtic Otherworld citadels are sometimes said to be made of glass and the Celtic name for Glastonbury according to an early charter (its 601 date is currently disputed) was Ynys-witrin, the Isle of Glass.

On a purely practical, historical level, if Arthur's base was at South Cadbury Hillfort and if he was killed there (there is a River Cam running near the hillfort after which the Battle of Camlann might have been named), Glastonbury was the nearest important Christian site for so famous a person to be buried. And his body might even have been taken part of the way by boat!

'How Sir Bedivere cast the sword Excalibur into the lake.' *Drawing by Aubrey Beardsley*

7 The French Romances and Courtly Love

There is little doubt that it was the *Roman de Brut*, written by the Norman poet Robert Wace in the mid-twelfth century, which inspired a whole genre of work, now called the Arthurian Romances.

The *Roman de Brut* was written for, and dedicated to, one of the richest and most powerful women in Europe, Eleanor of Aquitaine, then recently married to Henry Plantaganet, Count of Anjou, and patron of both Robert Wace and Geoffrey of Monmouth.

Queen Eleanor lived in an age which saw the emergence of French cultural identity. The church (and its Latin culture) was central to this development and many of the abbey and cathedral schools in Burgundy and Normandy such as Chartres, Paris, Auxerre, Poitiers, Rheims and Tours had already become established centres of learning. But it was in the great French-speaking courts, and with royal and aristocratic patronage, that French popular culture in its two spoken languages (the *langue d'oc* of the south, and the *langue d'oil* of the north) was encouraged and romances written. The word romance indicates a work written in old French, itself a development of a dialect of the Roman language, Latin. And it was particularly in the courts of Eleanor and her children that the new romances of Arthur and his knights began to be written and presented as popular court entertainments.

Before the advent of the Romances in the mid-twelfth century literary entertainments at court consisted mainly of heroic types of narrative and great epic poems of military heroes, the *chansons de geste*, which glorified religious and tribal feelings and embodied ideas of nobility and feudal allegiance. The new Romances which displaced them had a different focus although they continued to reflect heroic codes of behaviour. They were usually presented as an episodic series of tales with descriptions of glittering tournaments or quests undertaken to save a lady, in which were mirrored a courtly and chivalric age with a specific ideal of exquisite manners and civility. They were additionally infused with the world of 'faery' – giants and dragons, illusory castles and beautiful women that had their home under water, magic spells and enchantments, elements drawn from the ancient mythological tales of the *conteurs*, the Celtic storytellers working in the French courts.

There was another difference which related to the way in which the poems were performed. The epic poem had been a ceremonial perform-ance, delivered in the great hall of castles before a mix of social classes, and recited in an exaggeratedly dramatic way. The new Romances (first written in verse until the thirteenth century, after which fashion dictated that they should be presented in prose form) were delivered in private rooms to a select and educated audience. The intimacy of such a gather-ing permitted variety of delivery, subtle nuances and levels of meanings. And a new element was introduced, foreign to the great epics which were macho tales of heroism and male camaraderie – love interest in the form of heterosexual liaisons, and directly inspired by the poems and songs of the troubadours working in the ducal courts of Provence.

The new Romances focused on the world of Arthur with little con-cern for historical accuracy. The warlord Arthur, who had brilliantly but temporarily halted the Anglo-Saxon conquest of western Britain in the mid-sixth century, was remodelled in these twelfth- and thirteenth-cen-tury poems and prose narratives into a chivalric king of the same chrono-logical period as his listeners. Arthur was provided with a personal history culled from ancient Celtic hero tales – an infancy shrouded in obscurity and ritualised, and fabulous events such as the withdrawal of the magic sword from the stone which proclaim his right to sacral kingship. As king of the Britons, according to the new tales, he spearheads victorious cam-paigns throughout Europe. His court, brilliant, aristocratic and Christian, is composed of twelve knights of the Round Table in imitation of Christ's twelve apostles. Two important elements in his story, again Celtic in ori-gin, are the rebellion and abduction of his queen by his sister's son, and Arthur's fatal wounding, after which he is ferried to an Otherworld isle ruled over by a trinity of queens where he awaits a second coming.

The court most associated with the development of the Arthurian Ro-mances is the great court of Troyes in Champagne which was presided over by Marie de Champagne, daughter of Eleanor of Aquitaine and Louis VI, and her husband, Henri, who gained an international reputation through expensively staged 'jousting tournaments', which were gorgeous and brilliant entertainments as well as highly dangerous war games. The tournaments often lasted for several days during which the court went hunting and hawking; in the evenings the feasts were followed by dancing and entertainments by musicians and the court poets.

It was in this court that the greatest poet of the age, Chretien de Troyes (1135-83), composed a number of romance poems specifically on Arthurian themes for his patrons. He created an image of Arthur, King of the Britons and the Knights of the Round Table as chivalric noblemen in which the ideal heroic qualities of the man-at-arms – his aggressiveness and fierceness and unswerving allegiance to his feudal lord – were blended with gallantry, graciousness and Christian humility. Infused into this image was the concept of the courtly lover and courtly love.

Courtly love had its origins in the feudal courts of Provence at the end of the eleventh century and the beginning of the twelfth, where in the courts of Aquitaine, Auvergne and Poitou it became a favourite form of entertainment. These courts in the south of France, with their own form of French, the *langue d'oc* which differed from the language of the north, the *langue d'oïl*, had been culturally influenced by contact with their sophisticated Arabic neighbours in Moorish Spain. The professional entertainers at these courts, poets who wrote and recited tales in verse and prose to a musical accompaniment, and who were permitted to move from one castle to another to entertain the rich and high-born, were the troubadours. The poetry of the troubadours had initially focused on the fabulous or the praise and glorification of warrior heroes but, influenced by Arabic verse and cultural ideas, they evolved a new kind of poetry with which they will always be identified – erotic love poems with a spiritual overlay in which the focus was always the lady. In seductively persuasive and flattering language the lady's exquisite beauty, social superiority and moral virtues could be so exaggerated that she was presented in terms of a goddess, her lover at her feet, obedient to her every whim, an adoring and often abject worshipper. The language of religion was used to heighten the mood and suggest the sublimity of love.

The origin of courtly love is thought in part to be a parody of the relationship of a vassal to his feudal overlord, in which the vassal swore to obey, protect and serve his liege lord until death. In courtly love poetry, a knight had two lords – the god of love and the beloved lady. Accordingly the lady was often addressed in poetic terms as *mi dons* (my lord).

The idea that a woman should be idealised, idolised, pursued and courted by a man who was not her husband, even if ideal love was presented as platonic, was provocatively novel, especially in these early societies which purported to be fundamentalist Christians. There was also a potentially dangerous element in the tolerance of a courtly lover, for marriages at this social level were social and political contracts and rarely a matter of personal choice. For these reasons, it may be that, for the sophisticated and perhaps irreverent Provençal courts in the early twelfth century and later on the aristocratic societies of northern France, this kind of love was viewed as an amusing literary parody – of the feudal system, of the social system and of the Marian cult. There is no doubt that the church saw the dangers inherent in an expression of romantic love, which in its ideal form was platonic, the *amor de lohn* (love from afar) but, as illustrated by the popularity of the romance tales of Tristan and Lancelot, might encourage men and women to think of adulterous love as an accepted convention. It must also have been evident that the cult of the woman was in part a parody of the cult of the Virgin, for the lady is not simply exalted in the romances – she is often worshipped and prayed to and through her good grace can elevate a knight into an ecstatic 'heavenly state'. In some Romances a statue of the lady is worshipped in a shrine, and in Chretien's story of Lancelot, the knight on first being brought to the queen's bed genuflects and crosses himself as though Guinevere were a holy relic.

Marie is thought to have asked the chaplain Andreas Capellanus to codify the elaborate but unwritten rules governing the relations of courtly lovers as portrayed in troubadour poetry and the Romances. Capellanus obediently produced a work which, in the first two volumes, despite all its emphasis on politeness and respectful consideration of the lady, is evidently a parody of Ovid's bawdy *Ars Amatoria* (The Art of Loving) written in the first century BC. Andreas set out what appears to be the elaborate rules and certain of the case histories presented for adjudication in the courts of love presided over by Eleanor and her daughter and other great ladies, continually stressing the fact that romantic and sublime love cannot be experienced by a husband and wife – the love must be illicit. In the third volume of this treatise Andreas reveals what we probably have suspected – that the code of courtly love is not being set in cement, that the work is mock-serious, an elaborate literary joke and that as a priest he cannot condone adulterous behaviour.

The passionate love story of Tristan and Iseult first made an appearance in the French Romances in the twelfth century and achieved a startling popularity throughout Europe. Although the story of Tristan is thought to have been based on the ancient hero-tales of the Pictish dragon slayer

Drust or Drustan, the story was later remodelled to include love interest by adding elements from the ancient Irish tales of the warlord Finn, in particular those concerning the elopement of Finn's young wife Grainne with Diarmaid, one of Finn's élite warrior band, their flight and sojourn in a forest and the magic potion that bound them in love. The legend was further altered in the French Romances where Tristan is presented as a chivalric, feudal knight of Arthur's court as well as the courtly lover of Mark's queen.

The story of the adulterous relationship between Lancelot and Guinevere was the inspiration of Marie de Champagne who suggested to her court poet, Chretien, that Lancelot might be portrayed as a courtly lover enamoured of his queen. Until that moment Lancelot had played little part in the romance tales and had no relationship with Arthur's queen.

Chretien obligingly remodelled an old tale which he called 'The Knight of the Cart' and in which he portrays Lancelot as a very young knight of Arthur's court, skilled in the arts of war, kind, brave and noble, who at the beginning of the tale is embarking on a dangerous quest – to free the queen from the clutches of an evil lord who has spirited the queen away. Lancelot is taken through a series of extraordinary adventures which quickly reveal him to have all the hallmarks of the courtly lover as portrayed in troubadour and trouvere poetry (the trouveres were the poets working in the north). Lancelot's love is obsessive – he adores and idealizes the capricious queen, and he is prepared to suffer physical and mental pain, to lose face and even his life if it will serve his lady for he is determined to obey even her slightest whim. The Queen graciously rewards him by inviting him to share her bed. Chretien had little sympathy with adulterous love, but he shows the love to be a noble and elevating passion. When they return to court they are doomed to live the life of secret lovers, always at the mercy of the *losengiers*, the jealous slanderers at court, but Lancelot will to the end of his life be unswerving in his love and loyalty.

This then is the first of the Romance stories dealing with Lancelot as the Queen's champion and of their illicit relationship. It is also the first presentation of Guinevere as the *femme-dame*, the tricksy, capricious, wilful and passionate high-born lady who dares take one of her husband's knights as a courtly lover. Their relationship is to remain an important element in the Arthurian Romances and will be developed until it is recognised and presented as a factor in the overthrow of the Round Table and made the lovers, like Tristran and Isolde, bywords for tragic passion throughout Europe.

Hugely popular in their day, the Arthurian Romances remain a crucially important part of the ongoing process whereby the perceived world of Arthur was seamlessly and indelibly mutated from its legendary or obscure past into a period contemporaneous with the Continental and Anglo-Norman patrons who commissioned the stories as court entertainments for French speaking aristocrats.

8 The Quest for the Holy Grail

The tone and character of Arthurian Romances changed dramatically when in the late twelfth century and early thirteenth century the Christian warrior knights of Arthur's world now firmly established as Albion, were portrayed in romance literature as questing for a powerful, enigmatic and sacred object, the Holy Grail.

The word gra'al or graal (grail) during the medieval period did not have the same mystical connotation we give it today – for then it meant a serving dish or platter often of great worth designed to hold specially prepared food, a gastronomic delicacy, which was designated for the high table in a castle or great hall and carried by a young squire or a high servant with others in attendance with accompanying sauces. The gra'al then was not for daily use, and was reserved for secular and religious celebrations such as the birthdays and the saints' days of the noble company in addition to feast-days and the great church festivals of Christmas and Easter.

By dignifying the word gra'al with the epithet 'Holy', the more mundane meaning of a serving dish was changed to imply that the grail of the Arthurian romances was somehow a solemnly sanctified esoteric or devotional Christian cult object. In the wake of the crusades had come a great religious fervour and from the east a dissemination of objects associated with the life and death of Christ, such as the lance of Longinus claimed to have been found at the siege of Antioch in 1098 and which may be identified with the bleeding lance that often accompanies the grail in the Romances. Because of the contact with the Holy Land, the cathedrals of the Christian world had become storehouses of miracle-working relics all of which were believed to be imbued with *virtus* (virtue), a healing power inherited from connection with Christ and His saints. 'New' and fabulous saints' lives were written, presented and accepted as fact, although they had little to do with historical reality. Reflecting the new religious zeal, many monastic houses were reformed;

some new orders including the Cistercians placed an emphasis on the penitential life, with devotional exercises such as fasting, flagellation and other forms of mortification reflecting the practices of the desert fathers; while the idea of virginity, reflected in the cult of the Divine Mother, was elevated into a virtue. Religion and belief also played vital roles in the daily life of every man, woman and child.

Stories of the Holy Grail as a Christian cult object appeared for the first time in Europe in the latter half of the twelfth century. Confusingly there is no conformity of presentation which means that the grail must remain forever an enigma object; for some grail writers it is specifically the dish from which Christ and his disciples partook of the paschal lamb at the Last Supper. For others, beginning with the Burgundian poet, Robert de Boron in the late twelfth century, it was a reliquary, for it is claimed that it is the dish of the Last Supper used by Joseph of Arimathea to catch the blood droplets from the wounds of the dying Christ as He hung on the cross. In these stories Joseph of Arimathea, who is briefly mentioned in the gospels as having given Christ burial, is said to have taken these sacred relics taken to England. His descendants are the royal guardians of the grail in the grail castle, Corbenic, who await the coming of the ultimate keeper of the grail – an elect knight of Arthur's British court.

No matter how ambiguous the description, these tales of the Sant Gra'al (the Holy Grail) are uniquely set, not in an historic, but in the mythical Arthurian world of romance, and uniquely involve the great knights of Arthur's British court. The grail tales became hugely popular in Europe; they were translated into a multiplicity of languages, and for generations had a profound and enduring effect on the Arthurian legend.

As the psychologist/folklorist Emma Jung has pointed out, part of the enduring interest in the Arthurian grail stories is due to the fact that 'they have many features and constants that are found in myths and fairy tales'. The grail, whatever its form (whether flat or deep dish, cup of the Eucharist or glass reliquary), emanates great light, and contains some mystical substance which maintains and preserves life. The grail is kept within a magically reappearing and disappearing castle which is usually sited near the sea or a river and which is intriguingly visible to only a very few of the Arthurian knights. The guardian of the grail castle, entitled the 'Fisher King' is ancient and grievously ill, having been pierced 'through his thighs', a suggested euphemism for castration. The countryside which surrounds the Fisher King's castle is a barren, blighted wasteland. If a great knight finds the castle and seeing the grail processed in the hall is inspired to ask a specific question, the king will be cured. Should the question not be posed the castle and all its company will dematerialise. If the errant knight perseveres in his quest for the grail he might be received into the castle a second time; then, if he asks the magic question, both the Fisher King and his land will be miraculously restored to health and fertility but from that moment on the knight will become the new Fisher King and the keeper of the grail.

The first version of this myth, this story of Christian knights from the Arthurian world questing for the Holy Grail, was Chretien de Troyes's *Perceval* written in 1190. In Chretien's long poem, only a few scenes are set in the British court at which king Arthur and his great entourage of famous knights are present for, the focus is on two young contrasting heroes whose adventures and experiences follow parallel courses; Perceval, the young rustic from Wales, starts off in the story as gauche and boorish, Gauvain is a stylish, sophisticated and chivalric courtier from Arthur's court. For Chretien, Perceval is the grail hero. Once he has left his mother's house in the foothills of Snowdon he is led mysteriously to the grail Castle. His varying adventures en route for the domain of the Fisher King involve life experiences in which he is educated in not only martial arts and social etiquette (which will befit him for aristocratic life at court), but also Christian observance and piety – all that was considered vital for the education of a Christian knight.

In the grail castle, Perceval watches tongue-tied as a strange procession enters the hall where he is being entertained. Leading the company is a youth carrying a white lance which is seen to bleed of its own accord. Two other lovely boys follow carrying branched candlesticks in which many candles are burning with a great intensity. Then comes a demoiselle, '*bele et gente et bien acesmee*' (fair and comely and beautifully adorned) carrying a glowing grail of the purest gold set with '*prescieuses pierres qui en mer ne en terre soient*' (the most precious gems of the earth and the sea). So great a light emanates from the grail that it eclipses all the lights in the hall.

Perceval stifles his intuitive wish to question the Fisher King about the procession and the grail and thereby fails to lift the spell from the castle, the mutilated king and his bewitched land. The following morning Perceval is excluded from the enchanted castle which then melts into the air. Chretien died before he had supplied an ending to this extraordinary work and other continuators finished his story. Chretien claimed that the subject matter of his poem was suggested by a book loaned to him from the library of his then patron, Philippe Count of Flanders, cousin and second husband of Marie de Champagne and Chretien's patron from 1180. Philippe was to lose his life in the third Crusade. The original manuscript that inspired Chretien's grail story has not been found but scholars suggest that the source book might have been a collection of ancient Celtic hero tales (notably those dealing with magic cauldrons of regeneration and horns of plenty, as well as the Irish *echtrai* which focused on fantastic journeyings) which Chretien remodelled and updated.

Amongst the very many grail romances which were written throughout the thirteenth century recasting the early grail stories of *Perceval*, and linking the mythological world of Arthur with Christianity, the most important and influential (indicated by the large number of surviving manuscripts in a number of European languages) was undoubtedly the mammoth anonymous French prose romance work which appears in five books but which is collectively known as the Prose Lancelot. *L'Estoire del Saint Graal*, though one of the last of the 'Lancelot' stories to be written, serves as a prologue to the cycle; it expands and enlarges Robert de Boron's tale by introducing Joseph of Arimathea's son, Josephe, who brings the holy grail to Britain as a missionary bishop. And in this version it is Joseph of Arimathea's grandson, Alain, who becomes the first Fisher King, and rules the grail castle known as Corbenic where the mysterious grail company awaits the coming of a great knight from Arthur's court.

The fullest book of this cycle, the *Lancelot*, deals with the greatest military knight of Arthur's court, Sir Lancelot de Lac, champion and lover of Arthur's queen, while the book which follows, *La Queste del Saint Graal* is the achievement of the grail by Lancelot's son, Galahad. In both these texts, the romance form becomes a vehicle for didactic moralising. Lancelot is a true and faithful vassal to his Lord, Arthur of the British, and a loving, obedient courtly lover dedicated to his Lady Guinevere. He has spent his life offering his services to the weak and oppressed, and has lived a good and noble life. But now a new kind of knight has emerged, the 'knight of Christ' suggested by the treatise *Liber ad Milites Templi: De Laude Novae Militae* (in praise of the new Knighthood) written in the early twelfth century by the Cistercian Abbott Bernard of Clairvaux. In this Bernard contrasts the knightly courtly lover ('are these the trappings of a warrior or are they not rather the trinkets of a woman?') with the members of the newly formed religious order, the Knights Templar, monk knights, only recently established in the Holy Land to protect pilgrims, an order in which 'deference is shown to merit rather than noble blood'. Now much more is demanded of the chivalric knight. Now there is a consideration of the grail hero's spirituality, with his life observed as a progress towards the godhead which in this, the most Christianised of the romance tales, takes physical form as the chalice of the mass holding the sacred person of the risen Christ.

In *La Queste del Saint Graal,* when the four grail-questing knights, Lancelot, Bors, Perceval and Galahad, leave the British court their adventures towards and inside the grail castle arre critically observed. Lancelot's martial prowess as a knight is undisputed, and he is a great chivalric hero, but his soul is seen to be besmirched through his adulterous liaison with the queen. His quest for the grail castle and his experiences there end in humiliation as he is revealed to be defiled and undeserving of the grail. Bors and Perceval are commended for their chaste lifestyle in text which is obsessively anti-feminist, while the young Perceval, in an excess of penitential zeal, mutilates (possibly castrates) himself to expiate for almost losing his virginity. It is Galahad's unflinching dedication to chastity in addition to his knightly qualities which enables him to achieve the grail, during which he experiences a beatific vision of the godhead after which he renounces the world and enters religion.

The singular story of Galahad must have been specifically written for the *Prose Lancelot* for it appears in no earlier grail text. The story of Galahad's conception is a particularly bizarre fabrication in that his mother Elaine (the lovely grail maiden and daughter of King Pelles, the Fisher King) permits Lancelot to take her virginity, in order to become pregnant and fulfil the prophecy that her child be born of the line of the Fisher kings and of the greatest knight in the world. As lover of the queen Lancelot will not lie with any woman other than Guinevere as this is against the accepted code of courtly love, but in the grail castle he is drugged with a magic potion before being lured to Elaine's bower and in a confused state lies with the grail maiden in the mistaken belief that she is Guinevere.

That the French *Prose Lancelot* at the beginning of the thirteenth century should focus on the grail as the Eucharist and stress the penitential, suggests that the Continental author or authors of these new Arthurian Romances were themselves in religion particularly as the works reflect the new scholastic interpretation of the eucharistic presence of Christ and of the sacramental principle following the doctrine of transubstantiation made at the fourth Lateran Council in 1215. At this Council, the mass was affirmed as a sacrificial sacramental rite, during which the bread and wine of the communion meal, while retaining their outward appearances, were transformed and became in verity the Saviour. At this same Council the Church authorised the sacrament of penance for all Christians which meant in effect that each Christian, in order to be fit to receive his Saviour in the eucharistic meal, was now obliged to confess his sins in secret to a priest at least once a year at Easter, and to receive absolution, carrying out the imposed penance in order to achieve a state of grace. Ian Bradley (*Celtic Christianity*, 1997, p.71) believes that *La Queste* must have been 'written by a Cistercian monk from the Champagne region between 1215 and 1230' as it so clearly 'reflects Bernard de Cluny's doctrine of grace and a mystical union with God'.

It appears that the monkish author of *La Queste del Saint Graal* desired his grail story to be the ultimate, for in his version a disembodied hand comes down from the heavens and removes the *Sant Graal* from the island of Britain and the world of Arthur.

9 Malory's *Le Morte D'Arthur* and the Tudor Myth

The superb French romances of the twelfth and thirteenth centuries led to a widespread cult of Arthurian romances throughout Europe, even extending to Icelandic sagas. As with the French romances, attention was diverted away from Arthur himself to the exploits of individual knights, thus giving a virtually unlimited fund of material.

An interesting feature in the North of England was the alliterative revival of the fourteenth century, when patriotic Arthurian romances were constructed in the archaic Old English metre, with an interesting blend of archaic diction and material with sophisticated 'state of the art' castles, tapestries, weapons, hunting techniques and so on. The finest of these is the anonymous *Sir Gawain and the Green Knight* which combines Celtic marvels with an entertainingly dramatic and ethical debate and brilliantly evocative and realistic descriptions of nature.

Another fine alliterative poem, *Morte Arthure* (*c.*1400), is one of the many sources of the finest of all the epics on Arthur's life, Sir Thomas Malory's *Le Morte D'Arthur*. There are both biographical and textual problems in studying Malory. From the *Morte* we learn that Malory is a 'knight prisoner' who has completed his work during the ninth year of the reign of Edward IV (1469-70). He has access to a large array of French Romances, which he is loosely translating for sections of his work; he is also using English sources and alliterative 'skeletons' (eg 'he gurde to sir Gawayne for greff of sir Gayus' and 'Kylle doune clene for love of sir Kay') creep into parts of his work.

Malory has a horror of civil war, which presumably reflects his own embroilment in the Wars of the Roses, and his prime requirement of kingship is a king who can protect his people from invasion and from civil broils by strong and just rule. Malory upbraids Englishmen (*sic*) for not supporting King Arthur against Mordred and then bravely draws a contemporary parallel which seems to refer to the mistreatment of Henry VI:

Lo ye all Englysshemen, se ye nat what a myschyff here was. For he that was the moste kynge and nobelyst knyght of the worlde, and moste loved the felyshyp of noble knyghtes, and by hym they all were upholdyn, and yet myght nat thes Englyshemen holde them contente with hym. Lo thus was the olde custom and usayges of thys londe, and men say that we of thys londe have nat yet loste that custom. Alas! thys ys a greate defaughte of us Englysshemen, for there may no thynge us please no terme.

The only knight Thomas Malory that we know of at this time is the Sir Thomas Malory of Newbold Revel in Warwickshire who was accused of a wide range of crimes, including rape, theft, assault, extortion and cattle rustling, and was a member of parliament! He spent some time in prison and was specifically excluded from several Yorkist pardons. He was buried in Greyfriars Church, Newgate in 1471, but this does not mean he was in prison at Newgate at the time as some writers have claimed; indeed the Lancastrian invasion of 1470 would make this unlikely. Peter Field's biography on the Newbold Revel Malory convinces us that he is the writer and explains the complexities and paradoxes of his political and ethical viewpoints.

Until this century Malory's work was only known through Caxton's printed edition, which he organised into twenty-one 'books' containing 507 chapters. But a manuscript of Malory was discovered at Winchester College in 1934, with a division into eight 'tales', which has been published by the Oxford University Press, edited by Professor Vinaver (most other editions continue to use Caxton's text). Close examination has shown that the Winchester manuscript is not the original one, but that it was in Caxton's hands for some years.

Malory's early life of Arthur is based on French 'Merlin' romances and has much 'Celtic' magic, including the conception at Tintagel and the Sword in the Stone. Arthur's legitimacy is doubted and this results in a civil war. Arthur also fights against the Roman Emperor Lucius, as in the account by Geoffrey of Monmouth. Separate books deal with the early adventures of Sir Lancelot and the adventures of Sir Gareth. Malory's treatment of the Tristram story and the Grail Quest are less interesting than his sources, though he does reduce the number of hermits in the Grail story and show a strong sympathy with Sir Lancelot.

The final two tales, *The Book of Sir Lancelot and Queen Guinevere* and *Le Morte D'Arthur,* are magnificent in their sympathetic treatment of the essentially well-meaning quartet of characters. Arthur, Guinevere, Lance-lot and Gawain are drawn into conflict against their wishes and the inter-ests of the country by a mixture of destiny, political intrigue, passion and and conflicting loyalties. It presents an epic tragedy in which the political manipulation of the love of Guinevere and Lancelot by Mordred and Aggravain hurtles Arthur's civilisation to destruction. The tragedy is ar-chetypal and all-embracing and Malory avoids the narrowly sexual focus which so belittles the great theme in Tennyson's *Idylls of the King*.

Lancelot and Guinevere are portrayed in vivid human terms, yet with enough of the courtly love relationship surviving from the French ver-sions to give Lancelot a fulfilment in the relationship which is lacking in Tennyson. Their dialogue is vividly humorous at times, more like a well-married couple than courtly lovers: 'Have ye no doute, madame, seyde sir Launcelot. I alow youre witte. Hit ys of late com syn ye were woxen so wyse!'

In *The Book of Lancelot and Guinevere*, time and again Lancelot suffers rebukes from Guinevere yet rescues her from all sorts of predicaments. In *Le Morte D'Arthur*, which directly follows on the previous tale to form an embryonic novel with consistent characterisation and themes, their liaison is formally proved to King Arthur (who has a 'deeming of it' but is ignoring it for political reasons).

> So thys season hit befelle in the moneth of May a grete angur and unhappe
> that stynted nat tylle the floure of chyvalry of ale the worlde was destroyed
> and slayne....ÓAnd all was longe uppon two unhappy knyghtis whych
> were named sir Aggravayne and sir Mordred.

Arthur thus has to take action as his family demand it and since the queen's action is a treasonable offence she is sentenced to death.

Lancelot's affair presents him with a dilemma of loyalty: should he rescue the Queen by fighting against his liege lord and fellow knights? Malory cleverly has Sir Bors (a respected figure, but not pro-Guinevere) to assess Lancelot's duty:

> I woll counceyle you, my lorde, that my lady quene Gwenyver, and she be
> in ony distres, insomuch as she ys in payne for youre sake, that ye knyghtly
> rescow her; for and ye ded ony other wyse all the worlde wolde speke you
> shame to the worldis ende. Insomuch as ye were takyn with her, whether

ye ded ryght othir wronge, hit ys now youre parte to holde wyth the
quene, that she be nat slayne and put to a myschevous deth. For and she so
dye, the shame shall be evermore youres.

Lancelot's response to this is: 'Now Jesu deffende me from shame.'

The rescue of Guinevere forges another link in the chain to disaster
for Lancelot inadvertently kills the unarmed Gareth and Gaheris (Gareth
having been knighted by Lancelot – another important bond which is
severed). Gawain had forgiven Lancelot the death of his brother Aggravaine because it was the latter's fault. He is, however, implacably determined to avenge his two younger brothers and requires the support
of his liege lord Arthur to attack Lancelot in his own lands abroad, thus
leaving the way open for Mordred's rebellion and the collapse of the
Round Table.

Malory puts the blame for this mainly on Mordred and Aggravaine.
But, as Arthur's death or disappearance approaches, Malory moves once
again into a Celtic realm of magic and mystery with the splendid scenes
of Bedivere returning the magic sword Excalibur to the Lady of the Lake,
and Morgan and her fellow queens carrying away the wounded king to
Avalon. Malory cleverly retains the mystery as a vital part of the story:

Thus of Arthur I fynde no more wrytten...nothir more of the verry ser-
taynte of hys dethe harde I never rede, but thus was he lad away in a shyp
wherein were three quenys...Yet some men say in many parts of Inglonde
that kynge Arthure ys nat dede, but had by the wyll of oure Lorde Jesu into
another place; and men say that he shall com agayne, and he shall wynne
the Holy Cross. Yet I woll nat say that hit shall be so, but rather I wolde sey:
here in thys worlde he chaunged hys lyff. And many men say that there ys
wrytten uppon the tumbe thys:

HIC IACET ARTHURUS
REX QUONDAM REXQUE FUTURUS

The English civil wars were symbolically ended by a re-enactment of
the myth of the return of Arthur with the Welsh Henry Tudor's victory
at Bosworth. Henry played on this myth by having his eldest son born at
Winchester and christened Arthur. Winchester was regarded by Malory
and Caxton as being Arthur's main capital as it had preceded London as

the capital of England and also because it housed what they thought was the original Round Table.

Stories featuring the Round Table usually have it seating about 150 knights and no indoor round table could easily do that. So the folklore sites for the Round Table – Caerleon Roman Amphitheatre, Mayburgh Henge, the Knot at Stirling Castle and Bossiney Mound – are outdoors. This accords with the Celtic idea of outdoor feasting and originates as a method to prevent squabbles over precedence.

The indoor Winchester Round Table is divided into only twenty-four segments, each bearing the name of an Arthurian knight, but it is still huge, weighing one and a half tons and being two and three-quarter inches thick. The Table is thought to be thirteenth century, but Henry VIII ordered its repainting for the entertainment of Queen Catherine's nephew the Emperor Charles V at Winchester in 1522. A large Tudor rose was added in the centre together with a painting of a bearded Arthur looking suspiciously like an older version of Henry VIII (who had recently grown a beard)!

Henry as a Tudor claimed descent from Arthur and after the death of his brother Prince Arthur he assumed his Arthurian mantle at tournaments etc and married his wife. Henry considered that he had a better claim to be Holy Roman Emperor through his descent via Arthur to Constantine the Great (according to the Tudor genealogists!) than Uncle Charles. Thus seating Uncle Charles beneath the newly designed and painted table was making a political point.

Polydore Vergil, Henry VII's official historian, turned against the Tudor-Arthurian propaganda and denounced the Arthurian stories as fiction during the reign of Henry VIII, the latter countered by encouraging the antiquarian John Leland to collect evidence of Arthur's existence: it is from Leland that we have the first details of the Arthurian folklore connected with South Cadbury Castle. Later in the Tudor period Edmund Spenser's *The Faerie Queene* also uses the Tudor myth that the return of the House of Arthur restores the glory of Britain. Spenser also links his allegory with the cult of Gloriana (Elizabeth I) who is sought by the hero Prince Arthur.

'Merlin and Nimme.' *Drawing by Aubrey Beardsley*

10 Tennyson and the Pre-Raphaelites

The seventeenth and eighteenth centuries had little Arthurian literature of merit, but the Romantic Movement with its renewed interest in the Middle Ages and the supernatural brought about a revival of interest in matters Arthurian. The republication of Malory's *Le Morte D'Arthur* in the early nineteenth century inspired both Alfred Tennyson and William Morris.

Tennyson was only in his early twenties when he wrote *The Lady of Shalott*, about his favourite topic of suspended animation. The story is connected to the Maid of Astolat story in Malory, but Tennyson uses an Italian medieval novelette, *Donna di Scalotta,* and introduces the curse, which is not in the English and French versions of the story. The Lady weaving sights from her mirror perhaps represents the ivory-tower poet or painter, but she is activated to defy the curse by the dazzling appearance of Lancelot in her mirror:

A bow-shot from her bower-eaves,
He rode between the barley-sheaves,
The sun came dazzling thro' the leaves,
And flamed upon the brazen greaves
Of bold Sir Lancelot.
A red-cross knight for ever kneel'd
To a lady in his shield,
That sparkled on the yellow field,
Beside remote Shalott.

All in the blue unclouded weather
Thick-jewell'd shone the saddle-leather,
The helmet and the helmet-feather
Burn'd like one burning flame together,
As he rode down to Camelot.

Some of the contemporary critics felt that the poem was not ethically sound in encouraging the Lady to break free from the curse, but allowing her to die as a result. We in the late twentieth century, with our greater understanding of the power of myth and symbol and of the workings of the subconscious mind, are more susceptible to the genre and to the dazzling effect of language and metre in this inspired poem. The late Pre-Raphaelite poet Waterhouse has two superb illustrations of this poem, one showing the Lady awakening into reality and the other showing her in the barge, preparing to die.

Tennyson's other main Arthurian work is a long blank verse epic, *Idylls of the King*, which consists of twelve stories published between 1856 and 1885. They were enormously popular in Tennyson's day, partly because the amazing Arthurian stories were relatively new to many of his readers and even in diluted form still fascinated them. But the *Idylls* lack the power of Malory, perhaps because Tennyson as Poet Laureate felt he had to give the stories an overtly moral framework and he ingeniously linked most of the problems in the stories to the adultery of Lancelot and Guinevere, which cankers the whole of society. This delighted the moral Victorians, but the breadth of Malory's vision is severely distorted by this treatment. And it must be admitted that Tennyson is variable when using the medium of blank verse.

The *Idylls of the King* shows a civilised society created from a brutish, chaotic and violent existence by a code of ideals imposed by Arthur on the Knights of the Round Table. Whilst they adhere to these principles his knights are able to control the bestial elements in their own nature and purge society. Animal imagery is used for anyone threatening the civilised fabric of society.

Tennyson agonised over writing the 'Holy Grail' idyll but eventually followed Malory in showing the weakening effect of the Grail Quest on the Round Table by draining much needed manpower:

'Ah Galahad, Galahad', said the King, 'for such
As thou art is the vision, not for these ...
A sign to maim this Order which I made ....
What are ye? Galahads – no, nor Percivales
but men
With strength and will to right the wronged.'

Tennyson seems to lose poetic interest in the these woodenly expressed moral ideas.

But the chief reason for the collapse of the Round Table is the adulterous relationship between Lancelot and Guinevere, the two individuals Arthur completely relies upon for support in establishing his society. Tennyson, by ingenious manipulation of his sources (well-researched and including Layamon and Lady Charlotte Guest's translation of *The Mabinogion*) shows in the individual idylls how the 'sullying of our Queen' threatens the happiness of Geraint and Enid and is partly responsible for the destruction of Balin, Merlin, Elaine, Pelleas and Tristram.

Merlin's perpetual life-in-death imprisonment was traditionally associated with his lust for a young enchantress (Vivien in some versions) but in Tennyson he really falls prey to despair because of the adultery, described in one of the better passages:

> Then fell on Merlin a great melancholy;
> He walked with dreams and darkness, and he found
> A doom that ever poised itself to fall,
> An ever-moaning battle in the mist ...

Tennyson (like William Morris who wrote his *Defence of Guinevere* in 1858) has some sympathy for the plight of Guinevere, who finds Arthur:

> ... Cold,
> High, self-contained, and passionless, not like him,
> Not like my Lancelot.

Arthur, confronted with the adultery, says to his wife:

> The children born of thee are sword and fire,
> Red ruin, and the breaking up of laws.

In true Victorian style Guinevere concedes: 'It was my duty to have loved the highest.'

The most powerful depiction in the poem is that of Lancelot, who lacks the fulfilment that Malory's Lancelot achieves in his courtly love relationship with Guinevere. Arthur cannot understand why Lancelot could not return Elaine's love:

> Who might have brought thee, now a lonely man
> Wifeless and heirless, noble issue, sons ...

But Lancelot is neither free to love her nor to reveal why:

> The shackles of an old love straitened him,
> His honour rooted in dishonour stood,
> And faith unfaithful kept him falsely true.

This is superbly expressed, but the weight of the adultery, the moralising and the cold figure of Arthur give an overtly Victorian flavour to the epic which is constricting. Much of the best poetry is in the final idyll, 'The Passing of Arthur', which was written much earlier in Tennyson's thirties as his *Morte D'Arthur*. It is mythological and magical and unconstrained by Victorian morality:

> ... King Arthur's sword, Excalibur,
> Wrought by the lonely maiden of the Lake.
> Nine years she wrought it, sitting in the deeps
> Upon the hidden bases of the hills.

> Then quickly rose Sir Bedivere, and ran,
> And, leaping down the ridges lightly, plunged
> Among the bulrush beds, and clutch'd the sword,
> And strongly wheel'd and threw it. The great brand
> Made lightnings in the splendour of the moon,
> And flashing round and round, and whirl'd in an arch,
> Shot like a streamer of the northern morn,
> Seen where the moving isles of winter shock
> By night, with noises of the Northern See.
> So flash'd and fell the brand Excalibur:
> But ere he dipt the surface, rose an arm
> Clothed in white samite, mystic, wonderful,
> And caught him by the hilt, and brandish'd him
> Three times, and drew him under in the mere.

By portraying the collapse of Arthur's Round Table on the shortest day of the year ('... that day when the great light of Heaven / Burn'd at his lowest in the rolling year'), Tennyson is cleverly linking Arthur's Empire into the cycle of natural growth and decay. By setting the battle at Lyonnesse ('A land of old upheaven from the abyss / By fire to sink in the abyss again'), Tennyson uses contemporary scientific knowledge to show that even the land itself is evolving and reforming like a social and political organisations – 'Lest one good custom should corrupt the world'.

The Pre-Raphaelite Brotherhood was interpreting Tennyson's Arthurian poetry in art from as early as 1848. Rossetti contributed five illustrations, three of them on Arthurian themes, to the 1857 edition of Tennyson's *Poems*. The influence of Morris and Burne-Jones on the Pre-Raphaelites began to draw them more towards Malory (as Morris did not much care for Tennyson's Arthurian poetry). However, since Malory is Tennyson's principal source, it is sometimes hard to judge which writer the artists are interpreting. Certainly the tremendous Victorian enthusiasm for things Arthurian, which has continued throughout our century, was largely generated by Tennyson, who with characteristic generosity continued to draw people's attention to the greatness of Malory.

Tennyson was strongly supported for the Laureateship by Queen Victoria and Prince Albert and he became a neighbour of theirs on the Isle of Wight. They both admired and enjoyed Tennyson's poetry and Albert chose Arthurian themes for the new decorations in the House of Lords. After Albert's death the idylls were dedicated to his memory (Swinburne cruelly called them 'The Idylls of Albert') and along with Tennyson's other poetry they represented a patriotic pro-monarchy stance at a time when republicanism was being advocated in some quarters.

The enormous popularity of Tennyson's Arthurian poems coincided with great advances in literacy and education at the end of the nineteenth century. Many children from all sections of society were introduced to Tennyson's Arthurian poems at school and a whole range of children's prose works on the tales of King Arthur were published in the late nineteenth and twentieth centuries, based mainly on Tennyson and Malory. The most popular children's abridged editions were: Sir James Knowles's *King Arthur and His Knights* (1862); Sidney Lanier's *The Boy's King Arthur* (1880) and Alfred Pollard's *The Romance of King Arthur and His Knights of the Round Table* (1917).

Malory continued to be regularly reprinted including a number of illustrated editions. In 1893-94, J.M. Dent produced an edition of Malory with twenty-one full-page illustrations and 585 headings, borders, initials and ornaments by Aubrey Beardsley.

It was perhaps for the first time at the end of the nineteenth century that Arthur became a classless folk hero for all the British people as opposed to being a cultural symbol for the aristocracy and educated and a folk hero amongst the Celts. Certainly a lot of English (as opposed to Welsh and Cornish) Arthurian folklore seems to date (or was first collected) from this time. Even some Cornish sites, such as 'Merlin's Cave' at Tintagel, are directly traceable to the influence of Tennyson. And early editions of Ordnance Survey maps played their parts with the creation of a 'Tintagel' village and a 'Camelot' at South Cadbury.

The late nineteenth- and early twentieth-century enthusiasm for comparative mythology and mythological exposition of legendary texts led to many studies of the Celtic religious material in the Arthurian legends and particularly in the Grail texts. Jessie Weston's *From Ritual to Romance* (1920) is an influential analysis of the origins and development of the Grail legend which inspired the Grail Castle and Fisher King elements in T.S. Eliot's *The Waste Land* (1922). Eliot uses the 'Waste Land' of the Arthurian myth as a metaphor for the spiritually and intellectually maimed modern European civilisation. *The Waste Land* is of gigantic influence on English literature and of itself has assured the survival of the Grail cultural traditions.

The leading prose writer of Arthurian fiction in the first half of the twentieth century is generally agreed to be T.H. White, who wrote three novels in quick succession – *The Sword in the Stone* (1938), *The Queen of Air and Darkness* (1939) and *The Ill-Made Knight* (1940). These were eventually republished as a tetralogy, with a later novel, *The Candle in the Wind*, under the title of *The Once and Future King* (1958). Walt Disney produced an animated film on the first and most comic of the novels – *The Sword in the Stone* (1963) and the tetralogy inspired a musical, *Camelot* by Lerner and Loewe, with a film version in 1967. John Boorman's film, *Excalibur* (1981), perhaps owes more to White, Rosemary Sutcliff and Mary Stewart than has been admitted and perhaps less to Malory than is claimed.

T.H. White's books are loosely based on Malory, but have comedy admixed with the tragedy and many original features such an ugly Lancelot, an education of Arthur through animal lore and wisdom and the *deliberate* seduction of her half-brother by Morgause. These latter two aspects and the idea of the return of Merlin on the eve of the final battle at Salisbury (which comes in a posthumous fifth book – the *Book of Merlyn*) are used by Borman in *Excalibur*. A notable feature is White's daring and creative use of anachronism, such as Arthur's page Sir Thomas Malory, whom he sends away before the fatal Battle of Salisbury so that there will be someone left to tell the Arthurian story.

In the last forty years of the twentieth century, the emphasis in Arthurian fiction was both on realism – attempts to set Arthur back in a fifth/sixth century setting – and paradoxically to emphasise the Celtic supernatural elements. At the forefront is Rosemary Sutcliff's much-loved and admired novel *Sword at Sunset* (1963). For this novel, Rosemary Sutcliff goes back to the early chronicles to emphasise the battles against the Saxons, using Nennius's list of sites. Despite being confined to a wheelchair, Miss Sutcliff inspected possible sites aided by an experienced military campaigner and they worked out a campaign strategy which has subsequently influenced historians. She also tackled the ambivalent attitude of the Church to Arthur in the Saints' Lives, by showing Arthur defending the Church, but coming into conflict with them over matters such as billeting and consuming monastic food supplies after battles. She rehabilitates Ambrosius into the Arthurian story and uses the tradition of Maximus as inspiration – in these two aspects she is followed by several later novelists. She also avoids using the later legendary addition of Lancelot in her story, having Bedwyr as the lover of the Queen.

Mary Stewart's four Arthurian novels also make strong use of early chronicle sources. Her first three novels – *The Crystal Cave* (1970), *The Hollow Hills* (1973) and *The Last Enchantment* (1979) – use Merlin (a bastard son of Ambrosius in her novels) as storyteller. This is appropriate because of the bardic traditions of storytelling and because many of the medieval romances focus on Merlin's role in Arthur's education and kingdom. Her fourth Arthurian novel – *The Wicked Day* (1984) – has Mordred as story teller, with a uniquely sympathetic version of his viewpoint. The novels are well-constructed and have a convincingly practical handling of the Celtic magical themes.

John Arden and Margaretta D'Arcy completed a learned and powerful play on Arthurian and Celtic themes – *The Island of the Mighty* – in 1973. I was fortunate enough to see the Royal Shakespeare Company production before it was closed down because of a dispute. Although the play seems to have been intended as an attack on imperialism, it does generate dramatic sympathy for the beleaguered Arthur who tries to protect his people from invasion, civil war and chaos. Celtic religious themes are subtly interwoven and Arden cleverly introduces translations of actual Welsh Arthurian texts into the play. A further theme is the role of the bard, seen through conflicts between Taliesin, Merlin and the young Aneurin, who fails the Bardic test because he will not obey the rules, yet is successful as a popular poet/song-writer (depicted as a guitar-strumming singer-songwriter à la Bob Dylan in the Royal Shakespeare Company production). There is also an amusing treatment of King Pellam as a religious maniac (who regards Arthur as Antichrist) and how he becomes the Fisher King. I regard this play as the most underestimated of all the modern Arthurian works.

The interest in the historical Arthur both led to and was enhanced by the remarkable excavations at South Cadbury hillfort led by Professor Leslie Alcock in 1966-70. The antiquary John Leland was the first to draw attention to possible Arthurian connections with South Cadbury in his *Itinerary* (1542):

> At the very south end of the church of South-Cadbyri standeth Camallate, sometime a famous town or castle ... The people can tell nothing there but that they have heard say Arthur much resorted to Camalat.

South Cadbury is a Somerset hillfort of eighteen acres, some 500 feet above sea-level. In the sixteenth century the highest part of the plateau was known as 'Arthur's Palace'. Professor Alcock found evidence of an Arthurian period timber hall on this site, a re-fortification of the hillfort in the late fifth-century including a drystone wall about sixteen feet thick running round the three quarters of a mile perimeter of the hillfort and incorporating pieces of Roman masonry and a gate-house similar to those used by Roman auxiliary troops. South Cadbury seems to be a military and/or political centre of the fightback against the Saxons at the end of the fifth century and Leland does seem to have stumbled on a tradition with a genuine basis.

Professor Alcock's book *Arthur's Britain – History and Archaeology AD 367-634* (1971) was one of the first by a leading archaeologist or historian to take Arthur seriously as an historical figure and was and continues to be of enormous influence. It was followed by Dr John Morris's *The Age of Arthur* (1977) an erudite and ingenious attempt to write a sequential Arthurian history by drawing on a wide range of multidisciplinary data. Dr Morris was one of the first of the leading twentieth-century historians to be willing to consider cultural evidence from literature and folklore to aid historical interpretation. Refreshingly undogmatic, Dr Morris was willing to consider circumstantial evidence to assist in building an Arthurian historical framework which could be challenged and debated. Professor Alcock and Dr Morris brought Arthurian history back into the fold of serious academic historical debate. The popularity of Alcock and Morris's work provoked a re-analysis of their sources, and a new questioning of Arthur's existence by scholars such as David Dumville and N.J. Higham. Whilst providing helpful textual correctives and insights, particularly into Gildas and Nennius, and a critical questioning of some of John Morris's assumptions and conclusions, the new scholars were obsessive in the lengths they went to in order to discredit any possibility of a sixth-century Arthur. Christopher Gidlow's recent work *The Reign of Arthur* has, with historical knowledge and common sense, challenged Higham and Dumville and reasserted Arthur's historical claims.

Geoffrey Ashe and Richard Barber have been prominent among English scholars who have researched and popularised Arthurian literature and legends and their cultural significance in recent years. American scholars, such as Roger Loomis, have particularly specialised in Celtic mythological aspects of the Arthurian legends and a number of American novelists have explored these mythological themes. Most important is Marion Bradley's *The Mists of Avalon* (1982) which reflects late twentieth-century cultural phenomena such as feminism and neo-paganism, yet succeeds in vividly highlighting the Celtic religious elements which undoubtedly underlie the early Arthurian stories. *The Mists of Avalon* is told from the point of view of the women, particularly of Morgan, but, refreshingly in a feminist study, the women don't turn out any nicer than the men! The women's viewpoint on the Arthurian legends is long overdue, though both Tennyson and Morris tried it to a certain extent with Guinevere. Also impressive is the subtle treatment of the physical shifting of the Celtic Otherworld – the side-by-side existence of several layered Glastonbury/ Avalons which can be reached through knowledge or sometimes (and this is very Celtic) by chance. The novel handles themes, symbols, characterisation and politics very cleverly. Despite its excessive anti-Christian bias, tasteless neo-pagan orgies and a rather flabby middle-section, this novel is powerful enough to become a twentieth-century Arthurian classic and is already being studied on some University syllabuses.

And so the Arthurian novels continue – Nikolai Tolstoy, Stephen Lawhead, Bernard Cornwell ... a seemingly endless stream of re-workings of the magic that will very likely continue in some form until the end of Western civilisation:

> What place is there within the bounds of the Empire of Christendom to which the winged praise of Arthur the Briton has not extended? Who is there, I ask, who does not speak of Arthur the Briton, since he is but little less known to the peoples of Asia than to the Bretons, as we are informed by pilgrims who return from Eastern lands? The peoples of the East speak of him as do those of the West, though separated by the breadth of the whole earth. Egypt speaks of him, nor is the Bosphorus silent. Rome, queen of cities, sings his deeds, and his wars are known to her former rival, Carthage. Antioch, Armenia and Palestine, celebrate his feats.
>
> (Alanus, *c.*1170)

Gazetteer of Arthurian Sites

CORNWALL

BODMIN MOOR (SX 0767)

A number of Arthurian sites, such as 'Arthur's Chair' and 'Arthur's Oven' were identified by a twelfth-century writer, Hermann De Tournai (see chapter 5). See also 'Dozmary Pool' and 'King Arthur's Bed'.

BOSSINEY MOUND (SW 0688)

Early Norman motte. King Arthur's golden Round Table is said to emerge each Midsummer's Day and hover in the air. (Source Baring-Gould from local information.)

CARN MATH (SW 7140)

Flat-topped hill with tumuli. Reputed burial site of King Mark.

CASTLE-AN-DINAS (SW 9462)

Possible site of Dimilioc, stronghold of Gorlois, Duke of Cornwall. Also known as 'Arthur's Hunting Seat'.

CASTLE DORE (SX 1054)

Fortification of the historical ruler Conomarus, otherwise known as King Mark of Cornwall.

CASTLE KILLIBURY (SX 0173)

Iron age hillfort near Woodbridge which, according to Welsh poetic tradition, is an encampment of Arthur's, stormed by Medraut and from which he abducted Guinevere.

CHAPEL POINT (SX 0243)

Promontory in Mevagissey Bay from which Tristan leapt in an attempt to escape King Mark's wrath after his adulterous relationship with Queen Iseult had been discovered.

DOZMARY POOL (SX 1974)

Bleak pool on Bodmin Moor, claimed to be the one into which Bedivere threw Excalibur while Arthur lay dying.

KING ARTHUR'S GREAT HALL OF CHIVALRY (Tintagel)   (SX O588)
Built between 1929 and 1933 in Fore Street. The inspiration of Frederick Glass-
cock, it contains 'King Arthur's Hall' with oil paintings of Arthurian legends by
William Hatherell and 'The Hall of Chivalry' with a fine Round Table built of
different kinds of Cornish granite. There is an outstanding collection of nearly
one hundred stained glass windows on Arthurian themes by Veronica Whall,
many containing heraldic devices of the Knights. The site is well worth visiting
and includes a video showing and book shop.

KING ARTHUR'S BED (SX 2475)
Deep indentation in the granite rocky summit of Trewortha Tor on Bodmin
Moor, claimed to have once housed the body of King Arthur.

KING ARTHUR'S HALL (Bodmin Moor) (SX 1277)
Rectangular structure with low earthen walls and granite slab floor on King
Arthur's Downs, Bodmin Moor. Its early date nullifies its claim to be an Arthu-
rian Hall.

MARAZION (SW 5130)
Local belief that Arthur was transformed into a raven (mentioned as British tradition in Cervantes's novel *Don Quixote*).

MERLIN'S ROCK (SW 4625)
Prominent rock near the shoreline south of Mousehole village identified by
Merlin as landing site of a future invading force. In 1595 four Spanish galleons
anchored here, devastated the area and burnt Mousehole to the ground. The
tradition is later than the event.

ROCHE ROCK (SW 9860)
High crag topped by a ruined medieval hermitage. Possible sanctuary mentioned
by Anglo-Norman writer, Beroul, in which Tristan and Iseult sheltered with the
hermit Ogrin (in an earlier hermitage) when fleeing from King Mark.

ST LEVAN'S CHURCH (SW 3822)
Stunning coastal site, difficult for transport, just east of Land's End. In tradition
Merlin was responsible for cleaving a granite boulder in the south side of the
churchyard and predicting:

   'When with panniers astride,
   A pack horse can ride
   Through St Levan Stone
   The world will be done'

The same deed and prophecy are also attributed to St Levan, for whom the rock was said to be a favourite resting place.

ST MICHAEL'S MOUNT (SW 5130)
Spectacular causeway island approached at low tides from Marazion. The Trevelyan family legend regarded the mount as a remnant of the lost realm, Lyonesse.

ST NECTAN'S KIEVE (near Trethevy) (SX 0888)
Spectacular waterfall reputed to be where Arthur blessed the knights of the Round Table before they set out for the Quest of the Grail.

ST SAMSON'S CHURCH (Golant) (SX 1255)
According to the twelfth-century writer Beroul, this church was known to Mark, Iseult and Tristan.

SLAUGHTER BRIDGE (near Camelford) (SX 1185)
Legendary site of the mortal combat between Arthur and his son Mordred at the close of the Battle of Camlan, on the banks of the River Camel, according to Geoffrey of Monmouth. The legend may be confused with a battle fought here between Celts and Anglo-Saxons in 823AD. The site of the Battle of Camlann could be anywhere on the River Camel, e.g. Padstow, Wadebridge, Bodmin or Camelford.

TINTAGEL (see chapter 5) (SX 0588)
Marvellously romantic peninsula and the reputed birthplace of Arthur according to Geoffrey of Monmouth. It contains the shell of a thirteenth-century castle in the custody of English Heritage and evidence of an Arthurian-period trading centre. The plateau above the Castle contains the Castle Gardens, the foundations of a tenth-century church and 'Arthur's Footprint.' On the seashore is 'Merlin's Cave'. Both these names are only traceable to the nineteenth century.

TRETHEVY QUOIT (SX 259689)
Less than a mile north east of St Cleer, this prehistoric chambered tomb is also known as Arthur's Quoit.

TRISTAN'S STONE (near Fowey) (SX 1152)
Now sited on the Fowey-Lostwithiel road, this granite seventh-century monolith once stood near Castle Dore. It is inscribed to Drustan, son of Cunomorus (possibly Tristran son of King Mark).

WHITESAND BAY (SW 3627)
Near Sennen Cove village and where Arthur, in alliance with local kings, defeated Vikings – a chronological mix-up of traditions.

SOUTH & MIDLANDS

BARHAM DOWN (Kent) (TR 2051)
According to Malory, Modred engaged his father Arthur in battle here but Arthur's forces won the day.

BATH (Avon) (ST 7464)
Identified as the site of the Battle of Badon by Geoffrey of Monmouth. It is likely that the sixth-century chronicler Gildas and the ninth-century chronicler Nennius also consider this as Bath (see argument in chapter 4). The actual battle site is likely to be Little Solsbury Hill, a Celtic hillfort two miles to the north-east of Bath.

BRENT KNOLL (Somerset) (ST 3451)
Fortified hillfort in the Somerset levels near the Bristol Channel which may at one time have been an island. In legend Sir Idur, a young knight of Arthur's court, slew three giants here.

CARHAMPTON (Somerset) (ST 0042)
According to the *Life of St Carannog*, Arthur hunted but could not destroy a dragon that was ravaging the land. The saint banished the beast and in gratitude was granted land by Arthur on which to establish a church.

DOVER (Kent) (TR 3141)
According to Malory, Arthur's army fought Modred's troops at Dover and here Gawain died and was interred. Dover Castle contains an 'Arthur's Hall'.

DUNSTER (Somerset) (SS 9943)
The possible site for 'Dindraethou' where Arthur and the chieftain Cador were based, according to the *Life of St Carannog* (chapter 4).

GLASTONBURY (Somerset) (ST 4938)
Alleged site of Arthur's burial. Identified by Gerald of Wales with the Celtic Otherworld magic Isle of Avalon. Later legendary connections with Joseph of Arimathea and the grail. Chalice Well set in an attractive garden entered from Chilkwell Street has long been considered a centre for healing and recent tradition links it with the Grail. The Tribunal in the High Street houses finds from the Glastonbury and Meare Celtic Lake villages.

GUILDFORD (Surrey) (TQ 0049)
Considered by Malory to be Astalot. Here the Fair Maid of Astalot fell into a decline for love of Lancelot.

LIDDINGTON CASTLE (Wiltshire) (SU 2180)
Some historians consider this hillfort to be the site of the Battle of Badon.

LINCOLN (Lincolnshire) (SK 9771)

Nennius places several Arthurian battles in the Province of Lindsey (roughly modern Lincolnshire). There was a Roman fort at Lincoln on the Fosse Way, on the site of the present Norman castle and archaeological evidence indicates considerable military activity around the gatehouse in the Arthurian period (chapter 4).

MERLIN'S MOUNT, MARLBOROUGH (Wiltshire) (SU 1868)

Prehistoric tumulus, landscaped in the eighteenth century, in the grounds of Marlborough College. There was a suggestion that Marlborough was named after Merlin.

PORTCHESTER (Hampshire) (SU 6105)

A Roman Fort of the Saxon Shore and possible site of Battle of Llongborth in which, according to a Welsh poem, the Dumnonian king Geraint was slain and in which he was supported by Arthur's cavalry (chapter 4).

SOUTH CADBURY (Somerset) (ST 6225)

South Cadbury hillfort was re-fortified in the Arthurian period. Professor Leslie Alcock's excavations of 1966-70 found a timber hall on the site of the Arthur's Palace' of tradition, a Roman auxiliary style gate house and a drystone wall around the perimeter all from the Arthurian period.

WHITE TOWER, TOWER OF LONDON

Where Arthur dug up the head of Bran the Blessed, according to Welsh poetry. Here according to Malory, Guinevere took refuge when pursued by Modred who intended to ravish her.

WINCHESTER (Hampshire) (SU 4829)

Malory and Caxton thought that Winchester was Camelot and that King Arthur's Round Table, which still hangs on the wall of the Great Hall, was original. The table probably dates from the reign of Henry III, with Tudor additions (chapter 9).

WALES & THE MARCHES

ALDERLEY EDGE (Cheshire) (SJ 8578)

Here Arthur and his knights lie sleeping, awaiting the advent of a white horse that will carry them into the world of the present. A carved head above a nearby small 'wishing well' is reputed to be that of Merlin.

ARTHUR'S CAVE (Hereford) (SO5415)

This cave, sited in the hillside of Little Doward in the Wye Valley, was first inhabited in the Stone Age. The hill was once fortified and possibly re-fortified in the early Arthurian period. May be identified with Geoffrey of Monmouth's 'Castle of Genoreu' in which Vortigern was beseiged by Ambrosius. The village of Ganarew is nearby as is the Roman settlement of Ariconium, identified as Nennius's 'Ergyng', where Arthur's Amr was slain.

ARTHUR'S STONE, DORSTONE (Hereford & Worcester)(SO 3143)

Prehistoric burial chamber which has variously been described in legend as the burial site of Arthur, of a giant slain by Arthur, and of a rival king killed by Arthur.

ARTHUR'S STONE (West Glamorgan (SS 4990)

Granite megalithic chamber on Cefn Bryn ridge near Reynoldston .The huge capstone is called 'Arthur's Stone'. One legend portrays Arthur as a giant who when walking in south Wales discovered a pebble (the capstone) in his shoe and threw it away. It came to rest on two other monoliths, seven miles away on Cefn Bryn.

BARDSEY ISLAND (Gwynedd) (SH 1221)

Merlin was imprisoned in a house of glass here.

CAERLEON (Gwent) (4ST 3390)

Fortress of the Roman Second Legion. Possible site of Nennius's 'Battle of the City of the Legions' (chapter 4). One of Arthur's capitals in Welsh poetry, the Roman amphitheatre here has become known as 'Arthur's Round Table'. Here Arthur held his court in a city of great splendour, according to the twelfth-century chronicler Geoffrey of Monmouth.

CERRIG MELBION ARTHUR (Dyfed) (SN 1131)

Translated from the Welsh this means 'the stones of the sons of Arthur'. According to an ancient Welsh Arthurian tale, Arthur lost two sons in a great battle and legend has it that these two great standing stones in the Presely Mountains commemorate their death.

DINAS EMRYS (Gwynedd) (SH 6049)

Hill in the Snowdon area occupied during the Arthurian period. In legend it is where the British king, Vortigern, ordered a fortress to be built but two dragons, one red, one white, lived below the foundations and prevented its construction. The story tells how Merlin, then a child (in other accounts Emrys/Ambrosius) revealed in prophetic language the presence of the dragons which symbolically represented the great struggle of the Saxons against the British Celts.

LITTLE DOWARD (SO5316)

The hillfort of Little Doward is identified with Vortigen's castle of Genorue (there is a current village of Ganerew nearby). Just below the hillfort to the south-east is King Arthur's cave.

THE PILLAR OF ELISEG (Clwyd) (SJ 2044)

Broken and eroded cross shaft. Its ninth-century Latin inscription indicates that it was set up as a memorial to the princeling Eliseg, who claimed descent from King Vortigern.

THE NORTH

ARTHUR'S ROUND TABLE, MAYBURGH (Cumbria)   (NY 5228)

Neolithic or early Bronze Age causeway enclosure south of Penrith.

BAMBURGH (Northumberland (NU 1834)

Dramatically sited Norman Castle on a volcanic plug which was built on earlier Celtic then Anglian fortified site. The Celtic name was 'Din Guayrdi'; Malory identifies Bamburgh (or Alnwick) with Lancelot's 'Joyous Garde', where Lancelot was buried.

CARLISLE (Cumbria) (NY 3955)

One of Arthur's principal courts in the literary tradition. Here Guinevere was brought to the stake because of her adultery with Lancelot. Setting for a popular Arthurian ballad *The Loathly Lady* in which Gawain marries an old hag who fortunately transforms on their wedding night into a beautiful young woman. The site of Nennius's seventh battle (Coit Celidon) was somewhere to the north of the city.

HIGH ROCHESTER (Northumberland) (NY 8499)

Roman outpost fort (Bremenium) north of Hadrian's Wall – it has been suggested as a possible site for Nennius's eleventh battle.

PENDRAGON CASTLE (Cumbria) (NY 7802)

A Norman castle stands on the site of an earlier fort which local tradition claims was built by Uther Pendragon. Uther's attempt to divert the course of the River Eden and create a moat around the fortress failed (chapter 5).

SEWINGSHIELDS CRAGS (Northumberland) (NY 7970)

Arthur is said to sleep in a cave in the soaring whinsill which runs through the central section of Hadrian's Wall in Northumberland.

SCOTLAND AND THE BORDERS

ARTHUR'S SEAT, EDINBURGH (NT 2772)

Steep volcanic plug , a former hillfort, which rises above the city of Edinburgh. The earliest mention of its name was in the fifteenth century. Possible site of the 'mountain' Agned, Arthur's eleventh battle in Nennius.

BEN ARTHUR (Strathclyde) (NN 2505)
This mountain named after Arthur is in the Southern Highlands and rises to a
height of nearly 3000 ft.

CAERLAVEROCK (Dumfries) (NY 0454)
'The Fort of the Lark' – possession of which was the cause of the Battle of Arthuret
in which Merlin's lord, Gwendollau, was slain, causing Merlin's madness.

DRUMELZIER (Borders) (NT 1333)
Claimed to be the burial place of Merlin.

EILDON HILLS (Borders) (NT 5533)
The three rounded hills which dominate Melrose and the River Tweed have long
been thought the realm of the fairy folk and one of the many legendary places in
which Arthur and his knights lie sleeping.

LOCH LOMOND (Strathclyde/Central) (NS 3890)
Geoffrey of Monmouth describes how Arthur and his knights drove warring
Scots and Picts in their thousands onto the islands of Loch Lomond and held
them there in siege until they died of starvation.

MEIGLE (NO 2844)
Tayside, north-west of Dundee. In the Museum (formerly the churchyard) is
'Ganore's Grave', alleged tomb of Guinevere who in the local tradition was torn
to death by horses as a punishment for her adultery. There are a cluster of oth-
er Arthurian sites – 'Arthur's Fold', the 'Stone of Arthur' (standing stone) and
'Arthur's Seat' (see Glennie pp.37-40). Barry Hillfort is in local tradition that of
Ganore's abductor, Modred.

STIRLING (Central) (NS 7993)
Tilting ground now known as the 'King's Knot' was once called 'King Arthur's
Round Table'.

Notes and Acknowledgements

Thanks to Michael Symes for the suggestion of the title which Geoff used for a lecture at the Birkbeck Summer School at Westonbirt

PART ONE (chapters 1, 2 and 3)
Terry Lloyd
The chief sources for the historical section are: John Morris *The Age of Arthur*; Leslie Alcock *Arthur's Britain*; David Divine *North West Frontier of Rome*; David Breeze and Brian Dobson *Hadrian's Wall*; Peter Salway *Roman Britain* and N.J. Higham *The English Conquest*.

PART TWO (chapter 4-6, 9-11 Geoff Doel; 7-8 & Gazetteer Fran Doel)
Fran & Geoff Doel

4 THE MEDIEVAL WELSH SOURCES

For the chronicles of Gildas & Nennius, I have particularly used the editions in *The Arthurian Period Sources* series (vols 7 & 8 Phillimore). These give the Latin plus translation, but I have used my own translations in this book. For the commentaries on these texts I have been particularly influenced by John Morris *The Age of Arthur* (Weidenfeld & Nicolson 1973 and paperback in three volumes by Phillimore 1977), Leslie Alcock *Arthur's Britain* (Penguin 1971) and E.K. Chambers *Arthur of Britain* (1927: reprinted Cambridge 1964)

For *The Life of St Gildas* I should like to thank Llanerch Publishers and Hugh Williams for permission to quote from Professor Williams translation of Caradoc's *Life of Gildas* in *Two Lives of Gildas* (Llanerch).

For the discussion of Welsh poetry I am particularly indebted to E.K. Chambers *Arthur of Britain* (op. cit.). I should also like to thank Llanerch Publishers and Carl Lofmark for permission to use Professor Lofmark's translation of 'The Elegy For Gereint' in *Bards and Heroes* (Llanerch). My interpretation of this poem owes much to and quotes from Dr John Morris's analysis in *The Age of Arthur* (op. cit.).

Aneirin's *The Gododdin* is available in a scholarly edition edited by Kenneth Jackson (Edinburgh University Press) and a translation by Steve Short (Llanerch).

Selections from *The Black Book of Carmarthen* and *The Book of Taliesin* are available in text plus translation editions edited by Meirion Pennar (Llanerch). There is a selection of Arthurian Welsh hagiography, poetry and prose extracts with useful critical discussion *in The Celtic Sources for the Arthurian Legend* edited by Jon

Coe and Simon Young (Llanerch). Their book alerted me to references to Arthur in Breton Saints' lives.

In 1801 the antiquarian Edward Williams, also known as Iolo Morganwyd, published a collection of Welsh triads. Some are genuine, but some he seems to have written himself. Malcolm Smith has edited these in *The Triads of Britain* (Wildwood).

For *The Mabinogion*, good scholarly editions by Penguin and Everyman are available and my free 'literary' translations in this book are influenced by both.

5   GEOFFREY OF MONMOUTH AND TINTAGEL

My chief sources are Lewis Thorpe's Penguin edition of Geoffrey of Monmouth's *History of the Kings of Britain* and Professor Charles Thomas's *Tintagel: Arthur and Archaeology* (English Heritage/Batsford). But many of my suggestions and interpretations are original.

6   GLASTONBURY AND AVALON

My chief sources here are Leslie Alcock's *Arthur's Britain* (op. cit.) and Philip Rahtz's *Glastonbury* (Batsford/English Heritage) and *The Arthurian Encyclopedia* ed. Norris Lacy (Boydell).

7   THE FRENCH ROMANCES AND COURTLY LOVE

The relationship between the theory and practice of this kind of love ethic continues to be a matter of debate but R. Boase's *The Origin and Meaning of Courtly Love: A Critical Study of European Scholarship* (1977) and F.X. Newman's *The Meaning of Courtly Love* (1968) will prove helpful in any study of the subject, while A.K. Blumstein's *Misogyny and Idealisation in the Courtly Romance* (1977) gives a feminist interpretation of the subject.

Many of the various medieval texts of Tristan and Isolde are easily obtainable in Penguin translations nowadays, e.g. those by Eilhart von Oberge (1175), Beroul (1200) and Gottfried von Strassburg (1210).

8   THE QUEST FOR THE HOLY GRAIL

R.S. Loomis's *Arthurian Literature in the Middle Ages* provides an excellent introduction to the subject, while E. Kennedy's *Lanzelot and the Grail* (1986) and J. Frappier's contribution to *Grundriss der romanischen Literaturen des Mittelalters* (1978) provides valuable information into the roles played by Lancelot and his son in the development of the legend.

9   MALORY'S *LE MORTE D'ARTHUR* AND THE TUDOR MYTH

I have used Professor Vinaver's edition of Malory (OUP). Most of my analysis is original, but the section on the Round Table at Winchester is partly drawn from an article Fran & I wrote for the 'Keep' section of *The English Heritage Magazine*.

10 TENNYSON AND THE PRE-RAPHAELITES

I have used a number of editions of Tennyson's collected and selected poetry and specific editions of the *Idylls of the King*. The argument is substantially drawn from an unpublished research piece I submitted to Birkbeck College.

11 ARTHUR IN THE TWENTIETH CENTURY

Editions of the books and plays are given in the bibliography and I have drawn on the *Arthurian Encyclopedia* (ed. Norris Lacy) for specific details. The production of *The Island of the Mighty* I saw was by the Royal Shakespeare Company at the Aldwych Theatre in London in the 1970's.

ILLUSTRATIONS

All the site photographs were taken by Geoff Doel.

Bibliography

Alcock, Leslie 1971 *Arthur's Britain: History and Archaeology*, Harmondsworth: Penguin

Alcock, Leslie 1972 *By South Cadbury is that Camelot*, London: Thames & Hudson

Aneirin 1994 *The Gododdin* (ed. Steve Short), Felinfach: Llanerch

Arden, John and D'Arcy, Margaretta 1974 *Island of the Mighty*, London: Eyre Methuen

Ashe, Geoffrey 1980 *A Guidebook to Arthurian Britain*, London: Longman

Ashe, Geoffrey 1968 *The Quest for Arthur's Britain*, London: Pall Mall Press

Barber, Richard 1973 *King Arthur in Legend and History*, London: Cardinal

Beroul 1970 *The Romance of Tristan*, Harmondsworth: Penguin

Berthelot, Anne 1997 *King Arthur – Chivalry and Legend*, London: Thames & Hudson

Biddle, M. (ed.) 2000 *King Arthur's Round Table*, Woodbridge: Boydell

Boron, Robert de 2001 *Merlin and the Grail* (ed. Nigel Bryant), Cambridge: Brewer

Bradley, Marion 1982 *The Mists of Avalon*, Harmondsworth: Penguin

Chambers, E. K. 1927 *Arthur of Britain*, London: Sidgwick & Jackson

Coe, Jon and Young, Simon 1995 *The Celtic Sources for the Arthurian Legend*, Felinfach: Llanerch

Dark, K. R. 2000 *Britain and the End of the Roman Empire*, Stroud: Tempus

Dunning, R. W. 1988 *Arthur: The King in the West*, Stroud: Alan Sutton

Fairbairn, Neil 1983 *A Traveller's Guide to the Kingdoms of Arthur*, London: Evans Brothers

Field, Peter 1993 *The Life and Times of Sir Thomas Malory*, Woodbridge: Boydell & Brewer

Gantz, Jeffrey (ed.) 1976 *The Mabinogion*, Harmondsworth: Penguin

Gidlow, Christopher 2004 *The Reign of Arthur*, Stroud: Alan Sutton

Glennie, John 1994 *Arthurian Localities* (1869), Felinfach: Llanerch

Higham, N. J. 1994 *The English Conquest: Gildas and Britain in the Fifth Century*, Manchester: Manchester University Press

Higham, N. J. 2002 *King Arthur: Myth-Making and History*, London & New York: Routledge and Kegan Paul

Jackson, Kenneth 1969 *The Gododdin: The Oldest Scottish Poem*, Edinburgh: Edinburgh University Press

Lacy, N. J. (ed.) 1996 *The Arthurian Encyclopedia*, New York: Garland

Lapidge, M. & Dumville, D. (eds) 1984 *Gildas: New Approaches,* Woodbridge: Boydell & Brewer

Lofmark, Carl *Bards and Heroes*, Felinfach: Llanerch

Loomis, Roger (ed.) 1959 *Arthurian Literature in the Middle Ages*, Oxford: Clarendon Press

Loomis, Roger 1970 *The Development of Arthurian Romance* (1963), New York: Norton

Loomis, Roger 1992 *The Grail – From Celtic Myth to Christian Symbol* (1963), London: Constable

Malmesbury, William of, 1992 *The Antiquities of Glastonbury* (ed. Frank Lomax) (1908), Felinfach: Llanerch

Malory, Sir Thomas 1998 *Le Morte DArthur* (ed. Helen Cooper), Oxford: OUP

Matarasso, P. M. 1969 (ed.) *The Quest of the Holy Grail*, Harmondsworth: Penguin

Monmouth, Geoffrey of, 1966 *The History of the Kings of Britain* (ed. L. Thorpe), Harmondsworth: Penguin

Iolo Morganwg (Edward Williams) 1977 *The Triads of Britain* (ed. M. Smith) (1801), London: Wildwood

Morris, John 1973 *The Age of Arthur*, London: Weidenfeld & Nicolson

Morris, John (ed.) 1980 *Nennius, The British History and the Welsh Annals*, London & Chichester: Phillimore

Padel, O. 1984 'Geoffrey of Monmouth and Cornwall', *Cambridge Medieval Celtic Studies* 8: 1-28

Padel, O. 2000 *Arthur in Medieval Welsh Literature*, Cardiff: University of Wales

Pennar, Meirion (ed.) 1989 *The Black Book of Camarthen*, Felinfach: Llanerch

Pennar, Meirion (ed.) 1988 *Taliesin Poems*, Felinfach: Llanerch

Rahtz, Philip & Watts, Lorna 2003 *Glastonbury: Myth & Archaeology*, Stroud: Tempus

Tennyson, Alfred 1983 *Idylls of the King* (ed. J. M. Gray), Harmondsworth: Penguin

Thomas, Charles 1993 *Tintagel – Arthur and Archaeology*, London: Batsford

Tolstoy, Nikolai 1986 *The Quest For Merlin*, London: Hodder & Stoughton

Troyes, Chretien de 1991 *Arthurian Romances* (ed. W. Kibler), Harmondsworth: Penguin

Wace & Layamon 1962 *Arthurian Chronicles* (ed. G. Jones), London: Dent

Weston, Jessie 1920 *From Ritual to Romance*, Cambridge: CUP

Whittaker, Muriel 1995 *The Legends of King Arthur in Art*, Cambridge: Brewer

Williams, Hugh (ed.) 1990 *Two Lives of Gildas*, Felinfach: Llanerch

Winterbottom, Michael 1978 *Gildas – The Ruin of Britain and Other Works*, London & Chichester: Phillimore

Index

If you are interested in purchasing other books published by Tempus, or in case you have difficulty finding any Tempus books in your local bookshop, you can also place orders directly through our website www.tempus-publishing.com